Disclaimer

The information provided in this book, "SQL and Unity for 2D Game Development: A Hands-On Beginner's Guide," is intended for educational and informational purposes only. While every effort has been made to ensure the accuracy and completeness of[1] the content, the authors and publisher make no representations or warranties of any kind, express or implied, about the completeness, accuracy, reliability, suitability, or availability with respect to the[2] book or the information, products, services, or related graphics contained in the book for any purpose. Any reliance you place on such information is therefore strictly at your own risk.[3]

The authors and publisher shall not be liable for any loss or damage including without limitation, indirect or consequential loss or damage, or any loss or damage whatsoever arising from loss of data or profits arising out of, or in connection with, the use of this[4] book.

This book provides code examples and tutorials for interacting with SQL databases. It is the reader's responsibility to ensure that any code they implement is secure, efficient, and adheres to best practices for database management and security. The authors and publisher shall not be liable for any security vulnerabilities, data breaches, or other issues arising from the use of the code or techniques described in this book.

This book may contain links to external websites or resources that are not under the control of the authors or publisher. We have no control over the nature, content, and availability of those sites. The inclusion of any links does not necessarily imply a recommendation or endorse the views[5] expressed within them.

Software versions, libraries, and tools mentioned in this book may be subject to change or updates. It is the reader's responsibility to refer to the official documentation and resources for the latest information and compatibility.

The content of this book is protected by copyright laws. No part of this book may be reproduced, distributed, or transmitted in any form or by any means, including photocopying,[6] recording, or other electronic or mechanical methods, without the prior written permission of the publisher, except in the case of brief quotations embodied in critical reviews and certain other[7] noncommercial uses permitted by copyright law.

Every effort has been made[8] to ensure that the information provided in this book is accurate and up-to-date at the time of publication. However, the field of software development is constantly evolving, and new technologies, techniques, and best practices emerge regularly. The authors and publisher encourage readers to stay informed about the latest developments and advancements in SQL, Unity, and game development.

By reading and using this book, you acknowledge that you have read and understood this disclaimer and agree to its terms and conditions.

Introduction

Welcome to the exciting intersection of data and game development!

This book, "SQL and Unity for 2D Game Development: A Hands-On Beginner's Guide," invites you to unlock the power of data-driven game design. Imagine creating games where player choices shape the world, inventories dynamically adjust, and endless dungeons unfold with each playthrough. This is the magic you'll wield by combining the versatility of SQL databases with the creative engine of Unity.

Whether you're a budding game developer or an experienced Unity user seeking to expand your skillset, this book will guide you through the fundamentals of SQL and its seamless integration with Unity. We'll embark on a journey that starts with the basics of database design and culminates in building fully functional game projects.

What sets this book apart?

- **Hands-on Learning:** We believe in learning by doing. This book is structured around practical projects and real-world examples, ensuring you gain a deep understanding of how to apply SQL in your own games.

- **Beginner-Friendly Approach:** No prior SQL or advanced Unity knowledge is required. We'll guide you step-by-step, starting with the fundamentals and gradually introducing more advanced techniques.
- **Focus on 2D Game Development:** While many SQL concepts are universal, this book specifically tailors examples and optimizations for the unique challenges and opportunities of 2D game development.
- **Comprehensive Coverage:** From setting up your development environment to implementing online leaderboards and procedural generation, this book covers a wide range of topics to equip you with the skills you need to create truly dynamic and engaging games.

Get ready to:

- **Master SQL fundamentals:** Learn the language of data, from basic queries to advanced techniques like subqueries and aggregate functions.
- **Connect Unity and SQL:** Seamlessly integrate SQL databases into your Unity projects using C# scripts and libraries.
- **Build dynamic game systems:** Create persistent inventories, engaging quest logs, and branching dialogue systems using the power of data.

- **Generate procedural content:** Craft endless dungeons, unique items, and dynamic worlds with SQL-driven procedural generation.
- **Implement online features:** Build online leaderboards, player accounts, and shared game worlds.
- **Troubleshoot and debug:** Learn essential techniques to overcome challenges and ensure your data-driven games run smoothly.

This book is your gateway to a new level of game development, where data becomes a dynamic force driving player engagement and creativity. Join us on this exciting journey, and let's unlock the full potential of SQL and Unity to build the games of your dreams!

Part 1: Foundations

Chapter 1: Welcome to the World of Data-Driven Games

Why Use SQL in Unity? (Real-world examples: leaderboards, inventory systems, persistent worlds)

Imagine a game where every player has a unique journey, where worlds evolve based on their actions, and where content expands dynamically. This is the power of data-driven game development, and SQL is your key to unlocking it within Unity.

This chapter will introduce you to the exciting possibilities that arise when you combine the versatility of SQL databases with the creative engine of Unity. We'll explore why this combination is becoming increasingly essential in modern game development and how it can empower you to create richer, more engaging experiences.

Why Use SQL in Unity?

While Unity provides robust tools for building games, its built-in data handling has limitations, especially for complex or persistent data. This is where SQL shines. SQL (Structured Query Language) is a powerful language designed specifically for managing data in relational databases. By integrating SQL with your Unity projects, you gain the ability to:

- **Store and Retrieve Persistent Data:** Imagine a role-playing game where players can save their progress, inventory, and character attributes. SQL allows you to store this information in a database, making it accessible even after the game is closed and reopened. No more starting from scratch every time!

- **Create Dynamic Content:** Instead of hardcoding every item, quest, or level, you can store this information in a database. This allows you to easily update or expand your game's content without modifying the core code. Think of procedurally generated levels where the layout, enemies, and loot are pulled from SQL tables, creating a unique experience with every playthrough.

- **Build Online Features:** Leaderboards, player profiles, in-game messaging, and even massively multiplayer online (MMO) experiences rely on databases to manage user data, interactions, and game state. SQL provides the foundation for these online components.

- **Manage Complex Relationships:** SQL excels at handling relationships between different types of data. For instance, in a strategy game, you could use SQL to manage units, their attributes, their upgrades, and their relationships with other units, all within a structured and organized system.

Real-World Examples

Let's look at some concrete examples of how SQL is used in games you might already be familiar with:

- **Leaderboards:** Games like "Clash of Clans" or "Candy Crush Saga" use SQL databases to store player scores and rankings, creating a competitive environment and motivating players to strive for the top.
- **Inventory Systems:** "Diablo" and "World of Warcraft" rely on databases to manage complex inventory systems with hundreds of items, attributes, and crafting recipes.
- **Persistent Worlds:** MMORPGs like "EVE Online" and "Guild Wars 2" utilize SQL databases to store the state of the game world, including player positions, items, and even the history of events that have occurred.
- **Procedural Generation:** Games like "Minecraft" and "No Man's Sky" use algorithms to generate vast worlds. SQL can play a crucial role in storing the rules, parameters, and assets used in this generation process, allowing for near-infinite variations.

The Power of Data-Driven Design

By embracing SQL in your Unity projects, you're not just adding a database; you're opening the door to data-driven game design. This approach empowers you to:

- **Increase Development Efficiency:** Make changes and updates to your game more easily by modifying data rather than core code.
- **Improve Player Engagement:** Create personalized experiences, dynamic content, and online features that keep players coming back for more.
- **Scale Your Game:** Build games that can handle large amounts of data and many concurrent players.
- **Gain Valuable Insights:** Analyze player data stored in the database to understand player behavior, balance your game, and make informed design decisions.

In the following chapters, we'll delve deeper into the world of SQL, learn how to integrate it seamlessly with Unity, and embark on hands-on projects that will solidify your understanding and unleash your creative potential. Get ready to transform your game development process with the power of data!

Types of Databases and Choosing the Right One (SQLite vs. MySQL)

Now that you understand the benefits of using SQL in Unity, it's time to explore the different types of databases available and how to choose the right one for your game development project.

There are two main categories of databases:

- **Relational Databases:** These databases organize data into tables with rows and columns, forming relationships between different pieces of information.[1] They are excellent for structured data and complex queries.[2] Examples include MySQL, PostgreSQL, and SQLite.[3]
- **NoSQL Databases:** These databases offer more flexible data models and are often used for unstructured data, large datasets, and applications requiring high scalability.[4] Examples include MongoDB, Cassandra, and Redis.[5]

For most Unity game development projects, especially for beginners, **relational databases are the preferred choice**. They provide a good balance of structure, performance, and ease of use. Within this category, two popular options stand out: SQLite and MySQL.

SQLite: The Lightweight Champion

SQLite is a **file-based database** that is incredibly lightweight and easy to set up.[6] It stores all your data in a single file, making it highly portable and ideal for projects where simplicity and minimal overhead are crucial.[7]

Pros:

- **Ease of Use:** No server setup or configuration is required.[8] Just add the SQLite library to your Unity project, and you're ready to go.
- **Portability:** The entire database is contained in a single file, making it easy to share, back up, and deploy with your game.[9]
- **Performance:** SQLite is very efficient for read and write operations, especially for smaller datasets.[10]
- **Ideal for:** Mobile games, offline games, prototypes, and small-scale projects.[11]

Cons:

- **Limited Concurrency:** Not ideal for applications with many simultaneous users writing to the database.[12]
- **Scalability:** Performance can degrade with very large datasets.
- **Limited Features:** Lacks some advanced features found in server-based databases like MySQL.

MySQL: The Robust Workhorse

MySQL is a **server-based database** known for its reliability, scalability, and robust feature set.[13] It's a popular choice for web applications and larger-scale games.

Pros:

- **Scalability:** Handles large datasets and high user concurrency with ease.
- **Advanced Features:** Supports a wider range of SQL features, including user management, access control, and transactions.
- **Community Support:** Large and active community, providing ample resources and support.
- **Ideal for:** Online games, MMOs, games with complex data relationships, and projects that require high scalability.

Cons:

- **Setup and Configuration:** Requires setting up and managing a MySQL server, which can be more involved than using SQLite.[14]
- **Resource Intensive:** Can consume more resources than SQLite, especially with increased user load.

Choosing the Right Database

The choice between SQLite and MySQL depends on the specific needs of your game:

- **For simple games, prototypes, or mobile games with limited online features, SQLite is often the best starting point.** Its ease of use and portability make it a great choice for beginners.
- **If your game requires online features, handles a large amount of data, or needs to support many concurrent players, MySQL is the better option.** Its scalability and robust features make it suitable for more demanding projects.

Here's a quick decision guide:

Feature	SQLite	MySQL
Ease of Setup	Very easy	More involved
Portability	High	Lower
Performance	Excellent for small datasets	Excellent for large datasets
Scalability	Limited	High
Concurrency	Limited	High

| **Ideal for** | Offline games, mobile games, prototypes | Online games, MMOs, large-scale projects |

Ultimately, the best way to choose is to consider your game's requirements and your own comfort level. As you gain more experience, you can always switch to a different database system if your needs change.

Setting Up Your Development Environment (Step-by-step installation guides for Unity, database server, and necessary tools)

Before we dive into the exciting world of SQL and Unity, let's ensure you have a solid foundation by setting up your development environment. This involves installing the necessary software and tools to create, manage, and connect to your databases.

This guide provides step-by-step instructions for setting up your environment on Windows. If you're using macOS or Linux, the steps will be slightly different, but the core concepts remain the same.

1. Install Unity

- **Download Unity Hub:** Head to the official Unity website (unity.com) and download the Unity

Hub. This tool simplifies the installation and management of different Unity versions.

- **Install Unity Editor:** Open Unity Hub and click "Installs." Choose the latest LTS (Long-Term Support) version for stability. During installation, select the modules you need, such as platform support for your target devices (Windows, macOS, Android, iOS, etc.).
- **Create a New Project:** In Unity Hub, go to "Projects" and click "New." Choose a 2D template, give your project a name, and select a location to save it.

2. Choose and Install a Database Server

Based on our discussion in the previous section, you'll need to choose between SQLite and MySQL. Here's how to install each:

SQLite:

- **Download SQLite:** Visit the SQLite website (sqlite.org/download.html) and download the precompiled binaries for your operating system.
- **Add SQLite to Unity:** Extract the downloaded files and locate the sqlite3.dll file (for Windows). Create a Plugins folder in your Unity project's Assets directory and place the sqlite3.dll file inside it. This makes the SQLite library accessible to your Unity project.

MySQL:

- **Download MySQL Community Server:** Go to the MySQL website ([invalid URL removed]) and download the MySQL Community Server installer for your operating system.
- **Install MySQL Server:** Run the installer and follow the on-screen instructions. Choose a strong root password during the installation process.
- **Install MySQL Workbench:** MySQL Workbench is a visual tool for managing your MySQL databases. Download and install it from the MySQL website (dev.mysql.com/downloads/workbench/).

3. Install a Database Connector for Unity

To connect your Unity project to the database, you'll need a database connector library. Here's a popular option:

- **Mono.Data.Sqlite:** This library provides access to SQLite databases from within Unity. It's usually included with Unity, but if not, you can download it from the Unity Asset Store.

4. (Optional) Install a Code Editor

While Unity includes a built-in code editor, many developers prefer external editors for their enhanced features and customization options. Here are two popular choices:

- **Visual Studio Code:** A lightweight and versatile code editor with excellent Unity integration.
- **Visual Studio:** A full-featured IDE with powerful debugging and code analysis tools.

Verification

To make sure everything is set up correctly:

- **SQLite:** Create a new C# script in your Unity project and add the following code:

<!-- end list -->

```C#
using UnityEngine;

using Mono.Data.Sqlite;

using System.Data;


public class DatabaseTest : MonoBehaviour

{

    void Start()

    {
```

```
        string connectionString = "URI=file:" +
Application.dataPath + "/MyDatabase.db"; // Replace
with your database file path


        using (IDbConnection dbConnection = new
SqliteConnection(connectionString))

    {

        dbConnection.Open();

        Debug.Log("Connected to SQLite database!");

        dbConnection.Close();

    }

  }

}
```

Attach this script to a GameObject in your scene and run the game. If you see "Connected to SQLite database!" in the console, your SQLite setup is successful.

- **MySQL:** Open MySQL Workbench and connect to your MySQL server using the root credentials you created during installation. If you can connect successfully, your MySQL server is running correctly. You'll learn how to connect Unity to MySQL in later chapters.

With your development environment set up, you're ready to embark on your journey into the world of data-driven game development! In the next chapter, we'll delve into the fundamentals of SQL and learn how to communicate with databases.

Chapter 2: SQL Basics - The Language of Data

Understanding Databases, Tables, and Relationships

Imagine a database as a digital filing cabinet, storing and organizing information. Within this cabinet, you have drawers, each holding specific files. In the world of SQL, these drawers are called **tables**.

What is a Table?

A table is a structured set of data, organized into rows and columns. Each row represents a record, and each column represents a field. For example, in a game, you might have a table called "Players" with columns like "PlayerID," "Username," "Level," and "Score."

Relationships Between Tables

Often, different tables need to be connected to each other. For example, you might have a "Characters" table and an "Inventory" table. Each character can have multiple items in their inventory. This relationship is called a **foreign key**.

In this example, the "CharacterID" in the "Inventory" table is a foreign key that references the "ID" in the "Characters" table. This allows you to link items in the inventory to specific characters.

Common Types of Relationships:

- **One-to-one:** One record in one table corresponds to exactly one record in another table. (Example: A player can have only one account.)
- **One-to-many:** One record in one table can be associated with multiple records in another table. (Example: A player can have many items in their inventory.)
- **Many-to-many:** Multiple records in one table can be associated with multiple records in

another table. (Example: A player can be part of many guilds, and a guild can have many players.)

Understanding these relationships is crucial for designing efficient and effective database structures.

In the next section, we'll dive into the specific language of SQL, starting with the fundamental operations of creating, reading, updating, and deleting data (CRUD).

CRUD Operations: Creating, Reading, Updating, and Deleting Data

Now that you understand the basic structure of a database, let's learn how to interact with it using SQL. The core of this interaction revolves around four fundamental operations: **CRUD**.

CRUD stands for:

- **Create:** Adding new data to the database.
- **Read:** Retrieving data from the database.
- **Update:** Modifying existing data in the database.
- **Delete:** Removing data from the database.

Let's explore each operation with code examples and explanations, using a hypothetical "Players" table as our example. This table might have columns like "PlayerID," "Username," "Level," and "Score."

Create (INSERT)

To add a new player to our "Players" table, we use the
INSERT statement:

SQL

INSERT INTO Players (PlayerID, Username, Level,
Score)

VALUES (1, 'HeroGamer', 1, 0);

This code snippet inserts a new player with the specified
values into the "Players" table.

- INSERT INTO Players: Specifies the table to
  insert data into.
- (PlayerID, Username, Level, Score): Lists the
  columns where data will be inserted.
- VALUES (1, 'HeroGamer', 1, 0): Provides the
  corresponding values for each column.

Read (SELECT)

To retrieve data from the "Players" table, we use the
SELECT statement:

SQL

```
SELECT * FROM Players WHERE Username =
'HeroGamer';
```

This code retrieves all columns (*) from the "Players"
table for the player with the username "HeroGamer."

- SELECT *: Specifies that we want to retrieve all
  columns.
- FROM Players: Indicates the table to retrieve
  data from.
- WHERE Username = 'HeroGamer': Filters the
  results to only include the row where the
  "Username" is "HeroGamer."

You can also select specific columns:

SQL

```
SELECT PlayerID, Score FROM Players;
```

This would retrieve only the "PlayerID" and "Score"
columns for all players.

Update (UPDATE)

To modify existing data in the "Players" table, we use the
UPDATE statement:

SQL

```sql
UPDATE Players SET Level = 2, Score = 100 WHERE
PlayerID = 1;
```

This code updates the "Level" to 2 and the "Score" to 100 for the player with "PlayerID" 1.

- UPDATE Players: Specifies the table to update.
- SET Level = 2, Score = 100: Sets the new values for the specified columns.
- WHERE PlayerID = 1: Filters the update to only affect the row where "PlayerID" is 1.

Delete (DELETE)

To remove data from the "Players" table, we use the DELETE statement:

SQL

```sql
DELETE FROM Players WHERE PlayerID = 1;
```

This code deletes the player with "PlayerID" 1 from the "Players" table.

- DELETE FROM Players: Specifies the table to delete from.

- WHERE PlayerID = 1: Filters the deletion to only affect the row where "PlayerID" is 1.

Important Note: Always be careful with the DELETE statement, especially without a WHERE clause, as it can delete all data from a table.

These CRUD operations form the foundation of interacting with SQL databases. By mastering these commands, you'll be able to effectively manage your game data and create dynamic and engaging experiences for your players.

Common SQL Statements (SELECT, WHERE, ORDER BY, JOIN)

In the previous section, we introduced the fundamental CRUD operations. Now, let's delve deeper into some of the most common SQL statements you'll use to interact with your game's database.

SELECT: Retrieving Data

The SELECT statement is your primary tool for retrieving data from a database. It allows you to specify which columns and rows you want to retrieve.

Basic Syntax:

SQL

SELECT column1, column2, ...

FROM table_name

WHERE condition;

- SELECT column1, column2, ...: Specifies the columns you want to retrieve. Use * to select all columns.
- FROM table_name: Specifies the table to retrieve data from.
- WHERE condition: (Optional) Filters the results based on a specified condition.

Examples:

- Retrieve all columns from the "Items" table:

SQL

SELECT * FROM Items;

- Retrieve the "ItemName" and "Price" columns from the "Items" table:

SQL

SELECT ItemName, Price FROM Items;

- Retrieve all columns from the "Players" table where the "Level" is greater than 10:

SQL

SELECT * FROM Players WHERE Level > 10;

WHERE: Filtering Data

The WHERE clause allows you to filter the data retrieved by a SELECT statement. You can use various comparison operators and logical operators to define your conditions.

Comparison Operators:

- =: Equal to
- != or <>: Not equal to
- >: Greater than
- <: Less than
- >=: Greater than or equal to
- <=: Less than or equal to

Logical Operators:

- AND: Combines conditions[1] where both must be true.
- OR: Combines conditions where at least one must be true.
- NOT: Negates a condition.

Examples:

- Retrieve players with the username "NinjaGamer":

SQL

SELECT * FROM Players WHERE Username = 'NinjaGamer';

- Retrieve items with a price between 10 and 50:

SQL

SELECT * FROM Items WHERE Price >= 10 AND Price <= 50;

- Retrieve players who are not at level 1:

SQL

SELECT * FROM Players WHERE NOT Level = 1;

ORDER BY: Sorting Data

The ORDER BY clause allows you to sort the results of a SELECT statement based on one or more columns.

Syntax:

SQL

SELECT column1, column2, ...

FROM table_name

ORDER BY column1 ASC/DESC, column2 ASC/DESC, ...;

- ORDER BY column1 ASC/DESC: Specifies the column to sort by and the sorting order (ascending or descending). ASC is the default.

Examples:

- Retrieve players ordered by their score in descending order (highest score first):

SQL

SELECT * FROM Players ORDER BY Score DESC;

- Retrieve items ordered by price in ascending order (lowest price first), then by item name in alphabetical order:

SQL

SELECT * FROM Items ORDER BY Price ASC, ItemName ASC;

JOIN: Combining Data from Multiple Tables

The JOIN clause allows you to combine data from multiple tables based on a related column between them. This is essential for retrieving data that spans across different tables in your database.

Syntax:

SQL

SELECT column1, column2, ...

FROM table1

JOIN table2 ON table1.column = table2.column;

- JOIN table2: Specifies the second table to join.
- ON table1.column = table2.column: Specifies the condition for joining the tables, typically based on a common column.

Example:

Let's say you have a "Players" table and an "Inventory" table. You want to retrieve the username and the item name for each item in a player's inventory.

SQL

SELECT Players.Username, Inventory.ItemName

FROM Players

JOIN Inventory ON Players.PlayerID = Inventory.PlayerID;

This query joins the "Players" and "Inventory" tables based on the "PlayerID" column and retrieves the

"Username" from the "Players" table and the "ItemName" from the "Inventory" table.

Types of JOINs:

There are different types of joins (INNER JOIN, LEFT JOIN, RIGHT JOIN, FULL OUTER JOIN), each with its own specific behavior for handling unmatched rows. We'll explore these in more detail in later chapters.

Practice Problems

1. **Retrieve the names of all players who have a score greater than 1000.**

SQL

SELECT Username FROM Players WHERE Score > 1000;

2. **Retrieve the names of all items that cost less than 50 gold, ordered alphabetically.**

SQL

```
SELECT ItemName FROM Items WHERE Price < 50
ORDER BY ItemName ASC;
```

3. **Retrieve the usernames of all players and the names of the items they have in their inventory.**

SQL

```
SELECT Players.Username, Inventory.ItemName

FROM Players

    JOIN  Inventory  ON  Players.PlayerID  =
Inventory.PlayerID;
```

By practicing these SQL statements and exploring different variations, you'll gain a solid foundation for interacting with your game's database and unlocking the power of data-driven game development.

Data Types and Constraints (Ensuring data integrity)

Data integrity is crucial for maintaining a reliable and consistent database. It ensures that the data stored in your database is accurate, valid, and meaningful. This is where data types and constraints come into play.

Data Types

Every column in a SQL table has a specific data type. This defines the kind of data that can be stored in that column. Choosing the correct data type is essential for efficient storage and retrieval of information.

Here are some common SQL data types:

- **INTEGER:** For storing whole numbers (e.g., player level, item quantity).
- **REAL:** For storing decimal numbers (e.g., player health, item price).
- **TEXT:** For storing strings of characters (e.g., player name, item description).
- **BLOB:** For storing binary data (e.g., player avatars, item icons).
- **BOOLEAN:** For storing true/false values (e.g., is player online, is item equipped).
- **DATE:** For storing dates (e.g., account creation date, last login date).

- **TIME:** For storing time (e.g., time of last save, time of event).

Choosing the appropriate data type helps ensure that the data is stored correctly and efficiently. For example, storing a player's score as TEXT instead of INTEGER could lead to issues when trying to sort players by their score.

Constraints

Constraints are rules that you can apply to columns or tables to enforce data integrity. They help prevent invalid data from being entered into the database.

Here are some common SQL constraints:

- **NOT NULL:** Ensures that a column cannot contain a null value (e.g., a player must have a username).
- **UNIQUE:** Ensures that all values in a column are unique (e.g., each player must have a unique PlayerID).
- **PRIMARY KEY:** A combination of NOT NULL and UNIQUE. It uniquely identifies each row in a table (e.g., the PlayerID column in the Players table).
- **FOREIGN KEY:** Ensures that a value in one table matches a value in another table, establishing a relationship between them (e.g.,

the PlayerID in the Inventory table must refer to a valid PlayerID in the Players table).
- **CHECK:** Ensures that a value in a column meets a specific condition (e.g., a player's level must be greater than or equal to 1).

Example:

Let's say you're creating a "Players" table. You might define the following constraints:

- **PlayerID:** INTEGER, PRIMARY KEY (Ensures each player has a unique ID)
- **Username:** TEXT, NOT NULL, UNIQUE (Ensures each player has a unique username)
- **Level:** INTEGER, NOT NULL, CHECK (Level >= 1) (Ensures the level is a valid number)

By using constraints, you can prevent errors and inconsistencies in your data, making your game more robust and reliable.

Why Data Integrity Matters

Maintaining data integrity is crucial for several reasons:

- **Data Accuracy:** Ensures that the data stored in your database accurately reflects the real-world entities and relationships it represents.

- **Data Consistency:** Ensures that the data is consistent across all tables and relationships in your database.
- **Data Reliability:** Ensures that the data can be trusted for making informed decisions and providing a consistent player experience.
- **Game Stability:** Prevents errors and unexpected behavior caused by invalid or inconsistent data.

By understanding and implementing data types and constraints, you can create a robust and reliable database that forms the foundation of your data-driven game.

Chapter 3: Bridging the Gap: Connecting Unity and SQL

C# and Database Interaction (Introduction to libraries and APIs)

In the previous chapter, we explored the fundamentals of SQL and how to communicate with databases using SQL statements. Now, let's bridge the gap between your Unity game and your database by learning how to interact with it using C#.

The Role of C#

C# is the primary scripting language used in Unity. It provides the logic and functionality behind your game objects, interactions, and overall gameplay. To connect your C# scripts to a database, you'll need to utilize libraries and APIs (Application Programming Interfaces).

Libraries and APIs: Your Connection Tools

Think of a library as a collection of pre-written code that provides specific functionalities. An API defines how you can interact with that code, providing a set of rules and specifications for communication.

In the context of database interaction, libraries and APIs offer the following:

- **Database Connection:** Establish a connection between your Unity project and the database server (e.g., SQLite or MySQL).
- **Query Execution:** Execute SQL statements (like the CRUD operations we learned) from your C# code.
- **Data Retrieval:** Fetch the results of your queries and process them in your Unity game.
- **Data Management:** Handle data conversion, error handling, and other database-related tasks.

Common Libraries and APIs

Here are some commonly used libraries and APIs for database interaction in Unity:

- **Mono.Data.Sqlite:** This library provides access to SQLite databases from within Unity. It's often included with Unity, making it a convenient choice for beginners.
- **System.Data:** This namespace provides classes for accessing and managing data from various data sources, including databases. It's a core part of the .NET framework.
- **MySql.Data:** This library specifically enables interaction with MySQL databases. You'll need to download and install this library separately.

- **ODBC (Open Database Connectivity):** A standard API for accessing different database systems. It allows you to connect to various databases using a consistent approach.

Choosing the Right Library

The choice of library depends on the database system you're using and your specific needs:

- **For SQLite:** Mono.Data.Sqlite is the recommended choice due to its ease of use and integration with Unity.
- **For MySQL:** MySql.Data is the standard library for connecting to MySQL databases.
- **For other databases:** You might need to explore ODBC or other database-specific libraries.

Basic C# Code Example (SQLite)

Here's a simple example of how to connect to an SQLite database and execute a query using Mono.Data.Sqlite in C#:

Code snippet

```
using UnityEngine;

using Mono.Data.Sqlite;

using System.Data;
```

```csharp
public class DatabaseExample :
MonoBehaviour

{

    void Start()

    {

            string connectionString =
"URI=file:" + Application.dataPath +
"/MyDatabase.db"; // Replace with your
database file path


        using (IDbConnection dbConnection =
new SqliteConnection(connectionString))

        {

            dbConnection.Open();


            IDbCommand dbCommand =
dbConnection.CreateCommand();

            dbCommand.CommandText = "SELECT
* FROM Players"; // Your SQL query


            IDataReader reader =
dbCommand.ExecuteReader();
```

```
            while (reader.Read())

            {

                    // Process the data
retrieved from the database

                        string username =
reader.GetString(1); // Assuming "Username"
is the second column

                            int level =
reader.GetInt32(2); // Assuming "Level" is
the third column



                    Debug.Log("Username: " +
username + ", Level: " + level);

                }


            reader.Close();

            dbConnection.Close();

        }

    }

}
```

This code snippet demonstrates the basic steps involved in database interaction:

1. **Establish a Connection:** Create a connection object using the appropriate connection string.
2. **Open the Connection:** Open the connection to the database.
3. **Create a Command:** Create a command object to execute your SQL query.
4. **Execute the Query:** Execute the query and retrieve the results.
5. **Process the Data:** Read the data from the results and use it in your game.
6. **Close the Connection:** Close the connection to the database.

In the following sections, we'll delve deeper into these steps, explore different ways to execute queries, and learn how to handle various data types and scenarios.

Establishing a Connection (Step-by-step guide)

Connecting your Unity game to a database is the crucial first step in harnessing the power of data-driven game development. This section provides a detailed guide on establishing a connection, with code examples for both SQLite and MySQL.

1. Import Necessary Libraries

Before you can connect to a database, you need to import the required libraries into your C# script.

- **For SQLite:**

Code snippet

```
using Mono.Data.Sqlite;

using System.Data;
```

- **For MySQL:**

Code snippet

```
using MySql.Data.MySqlClient; // Make sure you have the MySql.Data library installed

using System.Data;
```

2. Construct the Connection String

The connection string provides the necessary information for your Unity project to locate and connect to the database. It acts like a map, guiding your code to the correct destination.

- **For SQLite:**

Code snippet

```
string    connectionString    =    "URI=file:"    +
Application.dataPath + "/MyDatabase.db";

// Replace "MyDatabase.db" with the actual name of
your database file.
```

This connection string specifies that the database is an SQLite database (URI=file:) and provides the path to the database file, which is located within your Unity project's Assets folder.

- **For MySQL:**

Code snippet

```
string                    connectionString                    =
"Server=localhost;Database=mydatabase;User
ID=your_username;Password=your_password;";

// Replace the placeholders with your actual MySQL
server details.
```

This connection string specifies the MySQL server address (Server=localhost), the database name (Database=mydatabase), your username (User

ID=your_username), and your password
(Password=your_password).

3. Create a Connection Object

Using the connection string, you create a connection
object. This object represents the connection to your
database.

- **For SQLite:**

Code snippet

```
IDbConnection dbConnection = new
SqliteConnection(connectionString);
```

- **For MySQL:**

Code snippet

```
IDbConnection dbConnection = new
MySqlConnection(connectionString);
```

4. Open the Connection

Once you have a connection object, you need to open the connection to establish communication with the database.

Code snippet

```
dbConnection.Open();
```

5. (Optional) Test the Connection

It's good practice to test the connection to ensure that everything is working correctly. You can do this by adding a simple Debug.Log statement:

Code snippet

```
if (dbConnection.State == ConnectionState.Open)

{

    Debug.Log("Connected to database!");

}
```

6. Handle Exceptions

Connecting to a database can sometimes fail due to various reasons (e.g., incorrect connection string, database server not running). It's important to handle potential exceptions to prevent your game from crashing.

Code snippet

```
try
{
    // Code to establish and open the connection
}
catch (Exception ex)
{
    Debug.LogError("Database connection error: " + ex.Message);
}
```

Complete Example (SQLite)

Code snippet

```
using UnityEngine;
```

```csharp
using Mono.Data.Sqlite;

using System.Data;


public class DatabaseConnection : MonoBehaviour
{
    void Start()
    {
        string connectionString = "URI=file:" +
Application.dataPath + "/MyDatabase.db";


        try
        {
            using (IDbConnection dbConnection = new
SqliteConnection(connectionString))
            {
                dbConnection.Open();


                if (dbConnection.State ==
ConnectionState.Open)
```

```csharp
            {
                    Debug.Log("Connected to SQLite
database!");
                }


            dbConnection.Close();
        }
    }

    catch (Exception ex)
    {
        Debug.LogError("Database connection error: " +
ex.Message);
        }
    }
}
```

By following these steps, you can successfully establish
a connection between your Unity game and your chosen
database. This connection forms the foundation for all

your future interactions with the database, enabling you to store, retrieve, and manage your game data effectively.

Executing SQL Queries from Unity

Now that you've established a connection to your database, it's time to learn how to execute SQL queries from your Unity C# scripts. This allows you to perform actions like retrieving player data, updating inventory items, or saving game progress.

1. Create a Command Object

After opening the database connection, you need to create a command object. This object will hold your SQL query and execute it against the database.

Code snippet

```
IDbCommand dbCommand = dbConnection.CreateCommand();
```

2. Set the Command Text

Assign your SQL query to the CommandText property of the command object.

Code snippet

```
dbCommand.CommandText = "SELECT * FROM
Players WHERE Level > 10"; // Example query
```

3. Execute the Query

Depending on the type of query, you'll use different methods to execute it:

- ExecuteReader(): Use this for SELECT queries that return data. It returns an IDataReader object that you can use to iterate through the results.
- ExecuteNonQuery(): Use this for INSERT, UPDATE, and DELETE queries that don't return data. It returns the number of rows affected by the query.
- ExecuteScalar(): Use this for queries that return a single value (e.g., SELECT COUNT(*) FROM Players). It returns the value as an object.

Code Examples for Common Queries

Here are some code examples demonstrating how to execute common SQL queries from Unity:

- **Retrieve all players from the "Players" table:**

Code snippet

```
dbCommand.CommandText  =  "SELECT  *  FROM
Players";


IDataReader reader = dbCommand.ExecuteReader();


while (reader.Read())
{
    // Process each row of data
    int  playerID  =  reader.GetInt32(0);  //  Assuming
"PlayerID" is the first column
    string  username  =  reader.GetString(1);  //  Assuming
"Username" is the second column
    // ... and so on
}


reader.Close();
```

- **Insert a new player into the "Players" table:**

Code snippet

```
dbCommand.CommandText = "INSERT INTO Players
(PlayerID, Username, Level, Score) VALUES (2,
'NewPlayer', 1, 0)";


int rowsAffected = dbCommand.ExecuteNonQuery();


if (rowsAffected > 0)
{
    Debug.Log("Player inserted successfully!");
}
```

- **Update a player's score:**

Code snippet

```
dbCommand.CommandText = "UPDATE Players SET
Score = 200 WHERE PlayerID = 1";


int rowsAffected = dbCommand.ExecuteNonQuery();


if (rowsAffected > 0)
```

```
{

    Debug.Log("Score updated successfully!");

}
```

- **Delete a player from the "Players" table:**

Code snippet

```
dbCommand.CommandText = "DELETE FROM Players
WHERE PlayerID = 2";


int rowsAffected = dbCommand.ExecuteNonQuery();


if (rowsAffected > 0)

{

    Debug.Log("Player deleted successfully!");

}
```

- **Get the number of players in the "Players" table:**

Code snippet

```
dbCommand.CommandText = "SELECT COUNT(*)
FROM Players";


int                playerCount              =
Convert.ToInt32(dbCommand.ExecuteScalar());


Debug.Log("Number of players: " + playerCount);
```

Important Considerations

- **Parameterization:** To prevent SQL injection vulnerabilities, it's crucial to use parameterized queries. This involves using placeholders in your SQL query and providing the values separately. We'll cover this in more detail in a later chapter.
- **Error Handling:** Always include error handling (try-catch blocks) to gracefully handle potential database errors.
- **Closing Connections:** Make sure to close the database connection (dbConnection.Close()) when you're finished with it to release resources.

By mastering the techniques of executing SQL queries from Unity, you'll be well-equipped to build dynamic and data-driven games that offer engaging and personalized experiences for your players.

Handling Database Results in Unity (Fetching and displaying data)

Executing SQL queries is only half the battle. The real magic happens when you can effectively handle the results of those queries within your Unity game. This involves fetching the data returned by the database and then using it to drive dynamic content, update UI elements, or modify game logic.

1. Using IDataReader

When you execute a SELECT query using ExecuteReader(), it returns an IDataReader object. This object provides a way to access the rows of data returned by the query.

Think of IDataReader as a cursor that moves through the result set one row at a time. You can access the values in each row using methods like:

- GetInt32(columnIndex): Retrieves an integer value from the specified column index.

- GetString(columnIndex): Retrieves a string value from the specified column index.
- GetFloat(columnIndex): Retrieves a float value from the specified column index.
- GetBoolean(columnIndex): Retrieves a boolean value from the specified column index.
- **... and other methods for different data types.**

Example:

Code snippet

```
dbCommand.CommandText = "SELECT PlayerID, Username, Level FROM Players";


IDataReader reader = dbCommand.ExecuteReader();


while (reader.Read())
{

    int playerID = reader.GetInt32(0); // Accessing the first column (PlayerID)

    string username = reader.GetString(1); // Accessing the second column (Username)
```

```
    int level = reader.GetInt32(2); // Accessing the third
column (Level)


    Debug.Log("Player ID: " + playerID + ", Username: "
+ username + ", Level: " + level);

}


reader.Close(); // Always close the reader when finished
```

In this example, the while (reader.Read()) loop iterates through each row in the result set. Inside the loop, you can access the values of each column using the appropriate Get method.

2. Storing Data in Unity

Once you've fetched the data, you'll often want to store it in Unity data structures for later use. This might involve:

- **Creating custom classes:** Define classes that represent your data structure (e.g., a Player class with properties for PlayerID, Username, Level, etc.).
- **Populating lists or arrays:** Store multiple rows of data in lists or arrays of your custom classes.

- **Assigning values to variables:** If you're retrieving a single value, assign it directly to a variable.

Example (using a custom class):

Code snippet

```
public class Player
{
    public int PlayerID;
    public string Username;
    public int Level;
}


// ... inside your database interaction code ...


List<Player> players = new List<Player>();


while (reader.Read())
{
    Player player = new Player();
```

```
player.PlayerID = reader.GetInt32(0);

player.Username = reader.GetString(1);

player.Level = reader.GetInt32(2);


players.Add(player);
}
```

```
// Now you have a list of Player objects that you can use
in your game
```

3. Displaying Data in the Game

Finally, you can use the fetched data to dynamically update your game's UI or modify game behavior. This might involve:

- **Updating text elements:** Display player names, scores, or other information in Text UI elements.
- **Populating lists or grids:** Display inventory items, leaderboards, or other lists of data.
- **Modifying game object properties:** Change the position, appearance, or behavior of game objects based on database values.

Example (updating a Text UI element):

Code snippet

public Text usernameText; // Assign your Text UI element in the Inspector

// ... inside your database interaction code ...

dbCommand.CommandText = "SELECT Username FROM Players WHERE PlayerID = 1";

string username = (string)dbCommand.ExecuteScalar();

usernameText.text = "Welcome, " + username + "!";

This example retrieves the username of a specific player and displays it in a Text UI element.

By combining these techniques, you can effectively handle database results in Unity and create dynamic, data-driven game experiences that respond to player actions and provide personalized content.

Common Connection Errors and Troubleshooting (Debugging techniques)

Connecting to a database can sometimes be tricky. Even with the correct code, you might encounter errors that prevent your Unity game from establishing a connection. This section explores common connection errors, provides troubleshooting tips, and introduces debugging techniques to help you identify and resolve these issues.

Common Connection Errors

- **Incorrect Connection String:** A common culprit is a mistake in the connection string. Double-check for typos, incorrect paths (for SQLite), or incorrect server details (for MySQL). Ensure that the database file exists in the specified location (for SQLite) and that the MySQL server is running and accessible.
- **Missing Libraries:** If you're using external libraries like MySql.Data, make sure they are correctly installed and referenced in your project. Check that the DLL files are in the correct location (usually the Plugins folder within your Unity project's Assets directory).
- **Firewall Issues:** Firewalls can sometimes block database connections. If you're using a server-based database like MySQL, ensure that

the firewall allows connections on the port used by the database server (default port for MySQL is 3306).

- **Database Server Not Running:** For server-based databases, ensure that the database server is running. You can usually check this through the server's management interface or by trying to connect to it using a database client like MySQL Workbench.
- **Incorrect Credentials:** Double-check that the username and password provided in the connection string are correct. For MySQL, make sure the user has the necessary privileges to access the specified database.
- **Database File Locked:** If you're using SQLite and the database file is locked by another process, you might encounter an error. Make sure no other programs are accessing the database file.

Troubleshooting Tips

- **Check the Console:** Unity's console is your first line of defense. It often provides detailed error messages that can pinpoint the source of the problem.
- **Use** Debug.Log **Statements:** Add Debug.Log statements to your code to track the progress of the connection process. For example, log messages before and after opening the

connection, and log the connection state to see if it's successfully opened.

- **Simplify the Code:** If you have complex code, try simplifying it to isolate the connection logic. This can help you rule out other parts of your code as the source of the error.
- **Test with a Simple Query:** Once you establish a connection, try executing a simple query (e.g., SELECT * FROM Players) to verify that the connection is working correctly.
- **Consult Documentation:** Refer to the documentation for the database system and the libraries you're using. They often provide troubleshooting tips and solutions for common errors.
- **Online Resources:** Search online forums and communities for similar errors. Many developers have likely encountered and solved the same problems you're facing.

Debugging Techniques

- **Breakpoints:** Use breakpoints in your code editor to pause execution at specific points and inspect the values of variables. This can help you track the flow of the connection process and identify where the error occurs.
- **Step-Through Debugging:** Use your code editor's step-through debugging tools to execute

your code line by line. This allows you to observe the behavior of your code and pinpoint the exact line where the error happens.

- **Inspect Variables:** While debugging, inspect the values of variables related to the connection, such as the connection string, connection state, and error messages. This can provide valuable clues about the cause of the error.

- **Exception Handling:** Use try-catch blocks to catch exceptions and examine the details of the error. The exception message and stack trace can provide insights into the source of the problem.

By combining these troubleshooting tips and debugging techniques, you can effectively diagnose and resolve connection errors, ensuring that your Unity game can successfully communicate with your database.

Part 2: Building Blocks

Chapter 4: Saving and Loading Game Data

Serialization: Preparing Your Game Data for Storage (JSON, XML, binary serialization)

In the realm of game development, persistence is key. Whether it's preserving player progress, maintaining inventory systems, or storing world states, the ability to save and load game data is crucial for a seamless and engaging player experience. This is where serialization comes into play.

What is Serialization?

Serialization is the process of converting your game data—which might exist as complex C# objects, variables, and data structures—into a format that can be stored and retrieved later. Think of it as translating your game's information into a language that can be written to a file or transmitted across a network.

Why Serialize?

- **Persistence:** Save game data to files, allowing players to continue their progress later.
- **Data Transfer:** Transmit data across a network for online multiplayer games or cloud saving.

- **Storage Efficiency:** Represent data in a compact format, minimizing storage space.

Serialization Formats

There are various formats for serializing data, each with its own strengths and weaknesses. Here are three common formats used in Unity:

1. JSON (JavaScript Object Notation)

JSON is a lightweight, text-based data format that is easy to read and write for both humans and machines. It's widely used in web development and has become increasingly popular in game development due to its flexibility and ease of use.

Pros:

- **Human-Readable:** Easy to understand and debug.
- **Lightweight:** Efficient for data transfer and storage.
- **Widely Supported:** Many libraries and tools available for working with JSON in Unity.

Cons:

- **Can be Verbose:** May not be as compact as binary formats for large datasets.

- **Limited Data Types:** May require extra effort to serialize complex data structures.

Example:

JSON

```
{
  "playerName": "HeroGamer",
  "level": 10,
  "score": 1500,
  "inventory": [
    { "itemName": "Sword", "quantity": 1 },
    { "itemName": "Potion", "quantity": 5 }
  ]
}
```

2. XML (Extensible Markup Language)

XML is another text-based data format that uses tags to structure data. It's been a popular choice for data serialization for many years, but it's gradually being replaced by JSON in many applications.

Pros:

- **Structured Format:** Clearly defines the relationships between data elements.
- **Extensible:** Can be customized to represent various data structures.

Cons:

- **Verbose:** Often more verbose than JSON, leading to larger file sizes.
- **Can be Complex:** Parsing XML can be more complex than parsing JSON.

Example:

XML

```xml
<player>
 <playerName>HeroGamer</playerName>
 <level>10</level>
 <score>1500</score>
 <inventory>
  <item>
   <itemName>Sword</itemName>
   <quantity>1</quantity>
```

```
      </item>

      <item>

        <itemName>Potion</itemName>

        <quantity>5</quantity>

      </item>

    </inventory>

</player>
```

3. Binary Serialization

Binary serialization converts data into a raw binary format, which is typically more compact and efficient than text-based formats. However, it's not human-readable and can be more challenging to debug.

Pros:

- **Compact:** Efficient for storing large datasets.
- **Fast:** Serialization and deserialization are typically faster than text-based formats.

Cons:

- **Not Human-Readable:** Difficult to understand and debug without specialized tools.

- **Platform-Dependent:** Binary formats might not be compatible across different platforms.

Example:

While a binary serialized file doesn't have a human-readable representation like JSON or XML, it would essentially store the data in a compact sequence of bytes.

Choosing the Right Format

The choice of serialization format depends on your specific needs:

- **For simple data structures and human readability, JSON is often the preferred choice.**
- **If you need a highly structured format and extensibility, XML might be suitable.**
- **For large datasets and performance optimization, binary serialization can be beneficial.**

In the following sections, we'll explore how to implement serialization in Unity using different techniques and libraries, empowering you to save and load your game data effectively.

Player Profiles and Preferences (Storing user settings and progress)

Creating personalized experiences is a cornerstone of engaging game design. Players want to feel a sense of ownership and control over their in-game journey. This is where player profiles and preferences come into play. By leveraging SQL databases, you can store and manage this information effectively, providing a tailored and immersive experience for each player.

What to Store in a Player Profile

A player profile can hold a wealth of information, including:

- **Basic Information:** Username, player ID, account creation date, last login time.
- **Progress Data:** Level, experience points, current location, completed quests, achievements.
- **Customization:** Appearance options (e.g., character customization, chosen avatar), preferred controls, audio settings, language preferences.
- **Inventory:** Items collected, equipment, resources, currency.
- **Social Information:** Friends list, guild membership, in-game communication preferences.

- **Gameplay Statistics:** Playtime, achievements earned, enemies defeated, high scores.

Designing the Database Structure

To store player profiles, you'll typically create a Players table with columns corresponding to the information you want to store. Consider using appropriate data types and constraints (as discussed in Chapter 2) to ensure data integrity.

Example Table Structure:

Column Name	Data Type	Constraints
PlayerID	INTEGER	PRIMARY KEY
Username	TEXT	NOT NULL, UNIQUE
Level	INTEGER	NOT NULL, CHECK (Level >= 1)
Experience	INTEGER	NOT NULL
CurrentLocation	TEXT	

AvatarID	INTEGER	FOREIGN KEY referencing Avatars table
SoundVolume	REAL	
Language	TEXT	

You might also have separate tables for inventory, friends lists, and other related data, linked to the Players table through foreign keys.

Saving and Loading Player Profiles

To save player profiles, you'll need to serialize the relevant data into a suitable format (JSON, XML, or binary, as discussed in the previous section) and store it in the database. When the player loads their profile, you'll deserialize the data and populate the game with the saved information.

Example Code (Saving with JSON):

Code snippet

```
// Assuming you have a Player class with properties for
the player data
```

```
Player player = new Player();

// ... populate the player object with current data ...
```

```
string jsonData = JsonUtility.ToJson(player); // Serialize
to JSON
```

```
// ... use SQL INSERT or UPDATE query to store
jsonData in the database ...
```

Example Code (Loading with JSON):

Code snippet

```
// ... retrieve jsonData from the database using a
SELECT query ...
```

```
Player                    player                    =
JsonUtility.FromJson<Player>(jsonData); // Deserialize
from JSON
```

```
// ... use the loaded data to update the game state ...
```

Handling Preferences

Player preferences can significantly enhance the gaming experience. Allow players to customize controls, adjust audio-visual settings, and tailor the game to their liking. Store these preferences in the player profile and apply them when the game loads.

Example:

Code snippet

```
// In your Player class:

public float soundVolume;

public bool subtitlesEnabled;


// ... when loading the player profile ...

audioSource.volume = player.soundVolume;

subtitleDisplay.SetActive(player.subtitlesEnabled);
```

Security Considerations

When handling player data, especially sensitive information like usernames and passwords, prioritize security.

- **Hash Passwords:** Never store passwords in plain text. Use secure hashing algorithms to protect them.
- **Prevent SQL Injection:** Use parameterized queries to avoid SQL injection vulnerabilities.
- **Data Sanitization:** Validate and sanitize any user input before storing it in the database.

By implementing robust player profile management and providing customization options, you can create a more personalized and engaging experience for your players, fostering a stronger connection with your game.

Saving Game State (Checkpoints, inventory, world state)

Saving game state is essential for providing players with a sense of progress and allowing them to resume their gameplay seamlessly. Whether it's through checkpoints, saving inventory, or preserving the entire world state, effective state saving enhances the player experience and prevents frustration.

Checkpoints

Checkpoints act as milestones in a game, allowing players to resume from a specific point if they fail or need to take a break. They offer a safety net, preventing players from having to restart from the beginning every time.

Implementing Checkpoints:

1. **Identify Save Points:** Determine logical locations in your game to serve as checkpoints. These could be at the start of a level, after completing a challenging section, or at key narrative moments.
2. **Capture Relevant Data:** Decide what data needs to be saved at a checkpoint. This might include:
   - **Player State:** Player position, health, current level, experience points.
   - **World State:** State of interactive elements (e.g., doors open/closed, puzzles solved), enemy positions, active events.
   - **Inventory:** Items collected, equipment, resources.
3. **Serialize and Store:** Serialize the captured data into a suitable format (JSON, XML, or binary) and store it in the database, associated with the player's profile.
4. **Load Checkpoint Data:** When the player loads a checkpoint, retrieve the saved data from the

database, deserialize it, and restore the game state accordingly.

Example Code (Saving a Checkpoint):

Code snippet

```
// Assuming you have a CheckpointData class to hold the relevant data


CheckpointData checkpointData = new CheckpointData();

checkpointData.playerPosition = player.transform.position;

checkpointData.playerHealth = player.health;

// ... capture other relevant data ...


string jsonData = JsonUtility.ToJson(checkpointData);


// ... use SQL INSERT or UPDATE query to store jsonData in the database ...
```

Inventory

Saving and loading inventory data is crucial for maintaining player progress and allowing them to manage their collected items, equipment, and resources.

Implementing Inventory Saving:

1. **Represent Inventory Data:** Use appropriate data structures (e.g., lists, dictionaries) to represent the player's inventory. This might involve creating custom classes to hold information about each item (name, quantity, attributes, etc.).
2. **Serialize Inventory Data:** Serialize the inventory data into a suitable format. JSON is often a good choice for its readability and ease of use.
3. **Store in the Database:** Store the serialized inventory data in the database, associated with the player's profile. You might have a separate Inventory table linked to the Players table through a foreign key.
4. **Load Inventory Data:** When the player loads their game, retrieve the inventory data from the database, deserialize it, and populate the in-game inventory.

Example Code (Saving Inventory):

Code snippet

```
// Assuming you have an Inventory class and an Item
class

List<Item> inventoryItems = player.inventory.items;

string jsonData = JsonUtility.ToJson(inventoryItems);


// ... use SQL INSERT or UPDATE query to store
jsonData in the database ...
```

World State

In some games, especially those with persistent worlds or dynamic environments, you might need to save the entire world state. This can be more complex than saving individual elements like checkpoints or inventory.

Implementing World State Saving:

1. **Identify Savable Elements:** Determine which elements in your game world need to be saved (e.g., object positions, states, interactions).
2. **Design a Data Structure:** Create a data structure to represent the world state. This might involve

nested objects or custom classes to capture the relationships between different elements.

3. **Serialize and Store:** Serialize the world state data and store it in the database. Consider using efficient serialization techniques for large datasets.

4. **Load World State:** When the game loads, retrieve the world state data, deserialize it, and reconstruct the game world accordingly.

Challenges and Considerations:

- **Performance:** Saving and loading large world states can be resource-intensive. Consider using optimization techniques like incremental saving (saving only changes) or asynchronous loading to minimize impact on gameplay.

- **Complexity:** Managing complex relationships between world elements can be challenging. Design your data structures carefully to ensure efficient serialization and deserialization.

- **Versioning:** If your game evolves and the world state structure changes, you'll need to handle versioning to ensure compatibility with older save files.

By effectively implementing game state saving, you can provide players with a seamless and immersive experience, allowing them to pick up where they left off and explore your game world without interruption.

Best Practices for Data Persistence (Error handling, data validation, security)

Saving and loading game data is crucial, but ensuring the reliability, integrity, and security of that data is equally important. This section outlines best practices for data persistence, focusing on error handling, data validation, and security considerations.

Error Handling

Database interactions are prone to errors, such as connection failures, invalid queries, or data corruption. Robust error handling is essential to prevent these errors from crashing your game or corrupting player data.

- **Use Try-Catch Blocks:** Wrap your database interaction code in try-catch blocks to catch potential exceptions. This allows you to handle errors gracefully and prevent them from propagating through your game.
- **Log Errors:** Log error messages to the console or a log file to help you identify and debug issues. Include relevant information like the exception message, stack trace, and the specific query or operation that caused the error.

- **Provide User Feedback:** If an error occurs during saving or loading, inform the player with clear and informative messages. Avoid technical jargon and offer potential solutions or workarounds.
- **Handle Connection Failures:** If a connection to the database fails, attempt to reconnect or provide options for the player to retry later. Consider implementing offline modes or local caching to mitigate the impact of connection issues.
- **Data Recovery:** If data corruption occurs, have mechanisms in place to recover or restore data from backups. Consider using versioning or checksums to detect and handle data inconsistencies.

Data Validation

Data validation ensures that the data you save and load is valid, consistent, and adheres to your game's rules. This prevents unexpected behavior, exploits, or data corruption.

- **Validate Input:** Validate any player input or data received from external sources before storing it in the database. This includes checking for valid data types, ranges, formats, and constraints.

- **Sanitize Data:** Sanitize data to remove potentially harmful characters or scripts that could compromise your database or game.
- **Use Constraints:** Utilize database constraints (as discussed in Chapter 2) to enforce data integrity at the database level. This includes NOT NULL, UNIQUE, PRIMARY KEY, FOREIGN KEY, and CHECK constraints.
- **Data Type Validation:** Ensure that the data you're saving matches the expected data types in your database schema. This prevents errors during serialization and deserialization.
- **Cross-Field Validation:** Validate relationships between different data fields. For example, if a player's level is stored in one field, ensure that their experience points fall within the expected range for that level.

Security

Protecting player data is paramount, especially when dealing with sensitive information like usernames, passwords, and in-app purchases. Implement security measures to safeguard your database and prevent unauthorized access.

- **Hash Passwords:** Never store passwords in plain text. Use strong hashing algorithms (e.g., bcrypt, scrypt) to protect passwords from breaches.

- **Prevent SQL Injection:** Use parameterized queries or prepared statements to prevent SQL injection attacks. This involves using placeholders in your SQL queries and providing the values separately, preventing malicious code from being injected into your database.
- **Access Control:** Implement access control mechanisms to restrict access to your database. Use appropriate authentication and authorization techniques to ensure that only authorized users or processes can access and modify data.
- **Encryption:** Consider encrypting sensitive data both in transit (using SSL/TLS) and at rest (using database encryption). This adds an extra layer of protection against unauthorized access.
- **Regular Backups:** Perform regular backups of your database to protect against data loss due to hardware failures, software errors, or malicious attacks. Store backups in a secure location.
- **Stay Informed:** Keep up-to-date with security best practices and vulnerabilities related to your database system. Regularly update your database software and libraries to patch security holes.

By adhering to these best practices, you can build robust and secure data persistence systems that safeguard player data, prevent errors, and ensure a smooth and enjoyable gaming experience.

Chapter 5: Dynamic Content with SQL

Creating a Simple Inventory System (Database design, UI integration, adding/removing items)

Imagine a game where players can collect items, manage their equipment, and use resources to craft new items. An inventory system lies at the heart of such experiences, and SQL databases provide the perfect tool for managing this complex data. This section guides you through creating a simple inventory system, covering database design, UI integration, and the essential operations of adding and removing items.

Database Design

    1. **Items Table:**

Column Name	Data Type	Constraints		
ItemID	INTEGER	PRIMARY KEY		
ItemName	TEXT	NOT NULL		
Description	TEXT			
ItemType	TEXT		(e.g., "Weapon", "Armor", "Consumable")
Icon	BLOB		(optional, for storing item icons)
Stats	TEXT		(optional, for storing item attributes as JSON)

    2. **Inventory Table:**

| Column Name | Data Type | Constraints | |---|---|---| | InventoryID | INTEGER | PRIMARY KEY | | PlayerID | INTEGER | FOREIGN KEY referencing Players table | | ItemID | INTEGER | FOREIGN KEY referencing Items table | | Quantity | INTEGER | NOT NULL, CHECK (Quantity >= 0) |

This design allows you to store information about each item in the Items table and track the quantity of each item a player possesses in the Inventory table.

UI Integration

1. **Inventory UI:** Create a UI panel or window to display the player's inventory. This might involve a grid or list to show the items, along with slots for equipped items.
2. **Item Representation:** Represent each item in the UI with an icon, name, and quantity. You can fetch the icon and name from the Items table based on the ItemID stored in the Inventory table.
3. **Item Interaction:** Allow players to interact with items in the UI. This might involve dragging and dropping items, right-clicking for context menus (e.g., "Use", "Equip", "Discard"), or clicking to view detailed information.

Adding Items

1. **Acquire Item:** When a player acquires an item (e.g., by picking it up, purchasing it, or receiving it as a reward), check if the item already exists in their inventory.
2. **Update Inventory Table:**
   - If the item exists, use an UPDATE query to increment the Quantity in the Inventory table.
   - If the item doesn't exist, use an INSERT query to add a new row to the Inventory table with the PlayerID, ItemID, and a Quantity of 1.
3. **Update UI:** Refresh the inventory UI to reflect the added item.

Example Code (Adding an Item):

Code snippet

```
// Assuming you have variables for playerID and itemID


// Check if the item already exists in the inventory

dbCommand.CommandText = "SELECT Quantity FROM Inventory WHERE PlayerID = @playerID AND ItemID = @itemID";
```

```csharp
dbCommand.Parameters.AddWithValue("@playerID",
playerID);

dbCommand.Parameters.AddWithValue("@itemID",
itemID);


int                    quantity                    =
Convert.ToInt32(dbCommand.ExecuteScalar());


if (quantity > 0)

{

    // Item exists, update quantity

        dbCommand.CommandText = "UPDATE Inventory
SET Quantity = @quantity WHERE PlayerID =
@playerID AND ItemID = @itemID";

        dbCommand.Parameters.AddWithValue("@quantity",
quantity + 1);

        dbCommand.ExecuteNonQuery();

}

else

{
```

```
// Item doesn't exist, insert new row

    dbCommand.CommandText = "INSERT INTO
Inventory (PlayerID, ItemID, Quantity) VALUES
(@playerID, @itemID, 1)";

    dbCommand.ExecuteNonQuery();

}


// Refresh inventory UI
```

Removing Items

1. **Trigger Removal:** When an item needs to be removed (e.g., used, equipped, discarded, or sold), trigger the removal logic.
2. **Update Inventory Table:**
   - If the Quantity of the item is greater than 1, use an UPDATE query to decrement the Quantity in the Inventory table.
   - If the Quantity is 1, use a DELETE query to remove the row from the Inventory table.
3. **Update UI:** Refresh the inventory UI to reflect the removed item.

Example Code (Removing an Item):

Code snippet

```
// Assuming you have variables for playerID and itemID


// Check the item quantity
dbCommand.CommandText = "SELECT Quantity FROM Inventory WHERE PlayerID = @playerID AND ItemID = @itemID";

dbCommand.Parameters.AddWithValue("@playerID", playerID);

dbCommand.Parameters.AddWithValue("@itemID", itemID);


int                    quantity                =
Convert.ToInt32(dbCommand.ExecuteScalar());


if (quantity > 1)
{
    // Decrement quantity
```

```
    dbCommand.CommandText = "UPDATE Inventory
SET Quantity = @quantity WHERE PlayerID =
@playerID AND ItemID = @itemID";

    dbCommand.Parameters.AddWithValue("@quantity",
quantity - 1);

    dbCommand.ExecuteNonQuery();

}

else if (quantity == 1)

{

    // Remove item from inventory

    dbCommand.CommandText = "DELETE FROM
Inventory WHERE PlayerID = @playerID AND ItemID
= @itemID";

    dbCommand.ExecuteNonQuery();

}


// Refresh inventory UI
```

By combining these techniques, you can create a
dynamic and interactive inventory system that enhances

your game's depth and provides players with a sense of ownership and progression. Remember to consider additional features like item stacking, equipment slots, and crafting systems to further enrich your inventory management.

Building a Quest Log (Tracking objectives, rewards, and progress)

Quests provide purpose and direction in games, guiding players through the narrative and rewarding them for their accomplishments. A well-implemented quest log helps players stay organized, track their progress, and understand their objectives. Here's how to build a quest log system using SQL:

Database Design

1. **Quests Table:**

Column Name	Data Type	Constraints
QuestID	INTEGER	PRIMARY KEY
QuestName	TEXT	NOT NULL
Description	TEXT	
RewardXP	INTEGER	
RewardItemID	INTEGER	FOREIGN KEY referencing Items table

2. **Objectives Table:**

Column Name	Data Type	Constraints
ObjectiveID	INTEGER	PRIMARY KEY
QuestID	INTEGER	FOREIGN KEY referencing Quests table
Description	TEXT	NOT NULL
TargetAmount	INTEGER	(e.g., "Kill 10 goblins")
CurrentAmount	INTEGER	

3. **PlayerQuests Table:**

Column Name	Data Type	Constraints
PlayerQuestID	INTEGER	PRIMARY KEY
PlayerID	INTEGER	FOREIGN KEY referencing Players table
QuestID	INTEGER	FOREIGN KEY referencing Quests table
Status	TEXT	(e.g., "Not Started", "In Progress", "Completed")
CurrentObjectiveID	INTEGER	FOREIGN KEY referencing Objectives table

This design allows you to define quests with multiple objectives and track each player's progress on individual quests.

UI Integration

1. **Quest Log UI:** Create a UI panel or window to display the quest log. This might involve a list of

active quests, with details for each quest (description, objectives, rewards).

2. **Objective Tracking:** Display the current objective for each quest, along with a progress indicator (e.g., "3/10 goblins slain").

3. **Quest Status:** Clearly indicate the status of each quest (not started, in progress, completed).

4. **Rewards Display:** Show the rewards associated with each quest, such as experience points or items.

Tracking Progress

1. **Accepting a Quest:** When a player accepts a quest, add a new row to the PlayerQuests table with the PlayerID, QuestID, and a status of "In Progress".

2. **Updating Objectives:** As the player progresses through the quest, update the CurrentAmount in the Objectives table and the CurrentObjectiveID in the PlayerQuests table.

3. **Completing Objectives:** When a player completes an objective, check if it's the final objective for the quest. If so, update the quest status to "Completed" in the PlayerQuests table.

4. **Claiming Rewards:** When a player completes a quest, allow them to claim the rewards. Update the player's experience points or add the reward item to their inventory.

Example Code (Updating Objective Progress):

Code snippet

```
// Assuming you have variables for playerID, questID,
and objectiveID


// Update the current amount for the objective

dbCommand.CommandText = "UPDATE Objectives
SET CurrentAmount = CurrentAmount + 1 WHERE
ObjectiveID = @objectiveID";

dbCommand.Parameters.AddWithValue("@objectiveID"
, objectiveID);

dbCommand.ExecuteNonQuery();


// Check if the objective is complete

dbCommand.CommandText = "SELECT TargetAmount,
CurrentAmount FROM Objectives WHERE ObjectiveID
= @objectiveID";

IDataReader reader = dbCommand.ExecuteReader();

reader.Read();

int targetAmount = reader.GetInt32(0);
```

```
int currentAmount = reader.GetInt32(1);

reader.Close();


if (currentAmount >= targetAmount)

{

    // Objective complete, update PlayerQuests table to
move to the next objective or complete the quest

    // ...

}
```

Additional Considerations

- **Quest Givers:** Implement NPCs or other mechanisms for giving quests to players.
- **Quest Dependencies:** Create dependencies between quests, where one quest must be completed before another can be accepted.
- **Quest Abandonment:** Allow players to abandon quests if they choose to.
- **Dynamic Quest Updates:** Consider dynamically updating quest objectives or rewards based on player choices or world events.

By combining these techniques, you can create a comprehensive quest log system that enhances player engagement and provides a sense of purpose and accomplishment as they explore your game world.

Generating Dialogue from a Database (Branching conversations, character interactions)

Dynamic and engaging dialogue is essential for creating immersive narratives and believable characters. Instead of hardcoding every line of conversation, you can leverage SQL databases to store and retrieve dialogue dynamically, enabling branching conversations and complex character interactions.

Database Design

1. **Characters Table:**

Column Name	Data Type	Constraints
CharacterID	INTEGER	PRIMARY KEY
CharacterName	TEXT	NOT NULL

2. **Dialogue Table:**

Column Name	Data Type	Constraints
DialogueID	INTEGER	PRIMARY KEY
CharacterID	INTEGER	FOREIGN

KEY referencing Characters table | | DialogueText | TEXT | NOT NULL | | NextDialogueID | INTEGER | FOREIGN KEY referencing Dialogue Table (itself) | | Condition | TEXT | | (optional, for conditional dialogue)

This design allows you to associate dialogue lines with specific characters and link them together to create conversational flows. The NextDialogueID creates a linked list structure, enabling branching paths based on player choices or conditions.

Implementing Branching Conversations

1. **Dialogue Triggers:** Trigger dialogue sequences through player interactions (e.g., talking to an NPC, activating a cutscene).
2. **Retrieve Initial Dialogue:** Based on the trigger, retrieve the initial DialogueID from the database. This could be associated with the NPC or the specific interaction.
3. **Display Dialogue:** Display the DialogueText associated with the retrieved DialogueID in a dialogue box or UI element.
4. **Player Choice:** Present the player with choices for their response. Each choice can be linked to a different NextDialogueID in the database.
5. **Follow Dialogue Path:** Based on the player's choice, retrieve the corresponding

NextDialogueID and display the associated DialogueText. Continue this process until the conversation ends or a specific condition is met.

Example Code (Retrieving Dialogue):

Code snippet

```
// Assuming you have a variable for the currentDialogueID


dbCommand.CommandText = "SELECT DialogueText, NextDialogueID FROM Dialogue WHERE DialogueID = @dialogueID";

dbCommand.Parameters.AddWithValue("@dialogueID", currentDialogueID);


IDataReader reader = dbCommand.ExecuteReader();

reader.Read();

string dialogueText = reader.GetString(0);

int nextDialogueID = reader.GetInt32(1);

reader.Close();
```

```
// Display dialogueText in the UI

// ...


// Update currentDialogueID to nextDialogueID for the
next line of dialogue

currentDialogueID = nextDialogueID;
```

Conditional Dialogue

To add complexity and dynamism to your conversations,
you can implement conditional dialogue. This involves
adding a Condition column to the Dialogue table. The
condition could be a simple boolean check (e.g.,
"HasPlayerCompletedQuest") or a more complex
expression.

Example:

DialogueID	CharacterID	DialogueText	NextDialogueID	Condition
l	l	'Have you seen any	you	

goblins
around
here?"

2	2	'Yes, I saw a few near the old mine."	
3	1	'Thanks for the information '	NULL
4	2	'Actually, 5 need you help dealing with them Will you take on a quest?"	'HasPlayer Completed Quest = False"
5	2	'Great! Here's what you need to do..."	NULL

| 5 | 2 | 'You already nelped me with that hanks again!'" | NULL | 'HasPlayer Completed Quest = True" |

In this example, the NPC's dialogue changes depending on whether the player has completed a specific quest.

Additional Considerations

- **Voice Acting:** If your game uses voice acting, you can store audio clips in the database or link dialogue lines to external audio files.
- **Character Emotion:** Consider adding a column for character emotion or expression to dynamically change character animations or portraits during dialogue.
- **Localization:** If your game supports multiple languages, you can store translations of dialogue in separate tables or columns.
- **Dialogue Editors:** Explore tools or plugins that provide visual editors for creating and managing dialogue trees, making the process more intuitive.

By implementing a database-driven dialogue system, you can create engaging and dynamic conversations that respond to player choices, world states, and character relationships, adding depth and immersion to your game's narrative.

Common Mistakes and How to Avoid Them
(Data redundancy, inefficient queries)

As you embark on your data-driven game development journey, it's easy to fall into common traps that can hinder performance, create inconsistencies, and complicate your database management. This section highlights some of these pitfalls and provides guidance on how to avoid them.

Data Redundancy

Data redundancy occurs when the same piece of information is stored multiple times in your database. This can lead to:

- **Wasted Storage Space:** Redundant data consumes unnecessary storage space, potentially increasing costs and slowing down database operations.
- **Data Inconsistency:** If the same information is stored in multiple places, updates become more complex. If updates are not synchronized, inconsistencies can arise, leading to conflicting

information and unexpected behavior in your game.

- **Increased Maintenance:** Managing redundant data adds complexity to database maintenance and increases the risk of anomalies during data updates.[1]

How to Avoid Data Redundancy:

- **Database Normalization:** Normalize your database to organize data into logical tables and minimize redundancy. This involves breaking down large tables into smaller, related tables and establishing relationships between them using foreign keys.
- **Use Foreign Keys:** Instead of duplicating data across tables, use foreign keys to establish relationships. This ensures that data is stored only once and can be accessed from other tables through references.
- **Data Deduplication:** Periodically audit and clean up your database to identify and remove duplicate data entries.
- **Careful Data Entry:** Implement validation checks and data entry procedures to prevent duplicate entries, especially in systems that involve manual data entry.

Inefficient Queries

Inefficient queries can significantly impact game performance, causing lag, slow loading times, and a poor player experience. Here are some common causes of inefficient queries:

- **Lack of Indexing:** Indexes speed up data retrieval by creating a sorted structure for specific columns. Without proper indexing, the database has to scan the entire table, which can be slow for large tables.
- **Unnecessary Data Retrieval:** Retrieving more data than needed can slow down queries. Use the SELECT statement to specify only the columns you require.
- **Missing WHERE Clauses:** Without a WHERE clause, the database has to retrieve all rows from a table, which can be inefficient. Use WHERE clauses to filter the results and retrieve only the necessary data.
- **Complex Joins:** Joining multiple tables can be expensive, especially if the join conditions are complex or the tables are large. Optimize your database design and queries to minimize the number of joins and the amount of data processed.
- **Large Datasets:** As your game grows, the amount of data in your database will increase. Implement techniques like pagination or lazy loading to handle large datasets efficiently.

How to Avoid Inefficient Queries:

- **Use Indexes:** Create indexes on frequently queried columns to speed up data retrieval.
- **Optimize SELECT Statements:** Retrieve only the necessary columns and use WHERE clauses to filter data effectively.
- **Simplify Joins:** Optimize your database design and queries to minimize the number of joins.
- **Analyze Query Performance:** Use database profiling tools to analyze the performance of your queries and identify bottlenecks.
- **Database Optimization:** Regularly optimize your database by defragmenting tables, rebuilding indexes, and updating statistics.

By avoiding these common mistakes and implementing best practices for data management, you can create efficient and reliable data-driven games that provide a seamless and enjoyable experience for your players.

Chapter 6: Level Up Your Game with Advanced Techniques

Procedural Generation with SQL (Generating levels, maps, or items based on database data)

Procedural generation breathes life into games by creating diverse and unpredictable content. Imagine vast worlds, intricate dungeons, or unique items, all generated algorithmically based on data stored in your SQL database. This section explores how to leverage SQL to drive procedural generation, adding a new dimension of replayability and dynamism to your games.

Database Design for Procedural Generation

The design of your database depends on the type of content you want to generate. Here's a general structure for generating levels or maps:

1. **Tile Sets Table:**

Column Name	Data Type	Constraints
TileSetID	INTEGER	PRIMARY KEY
TileSetName	TEXT	NOT NULL
Environment	TEXT		(e.g., "Forest", "Cave", "Desert")

2. **Tiles Table:**

| Column Name | Data Type | Constraints |
|---|---|---| | TileID | INTEGER | PRIMARY KEY | | TileSetID | INTEGER | FOREIGN KEY referencing TileSets table | | TileType | TEXT | NOT NULL | (e.g., "Floor", "Wall", "Obstacle") | Sprite | BLOB | | (optional, for storing tile sprites) | Properties | TEXT | | (optional, for storing tile attributes as JSON)

3. **Level Templates Table:**

| Column Name | Data Type | Constraints |
|---|---|---| | TemplateID | INTEGER | PRIMARY KEY | | TemplateName | TEXT | NOT NULL | | TileSetID | INTEGER | FOREIGN KEY referencing TileSets table | | Layout | TEXT | | (e.g., a string representing the level layout) | Rules | TEXT | | (optional, for storing generation rules as JSON)

This structure allows you to define different tile sets, individual tiles within those sets, and level templates that use those tiles. The Layout column can store a representation of the level structure, while the Rules column can hold additional parameters or constraints for the generation algorithm.

Generating Levels or Maps

1. **Choose a Template:** Select a level template from the Level Templates table based on desired criteria (e.g., difficulty, environment).
2. **Retrieve Tile Set:** Retrieve the associated tile set from the Tile Sets table.
3. **Interpret Layout:** Interpret the Layout data from the template to determine the basic structure of the level. This might involve parsing a string representation or decoding a binary format.
4. **Populate with Tiles:** Populate the level with tiles from the Tiles table, following the layout and any additional rules specified in the template.
5. **Apply Variations:** Introduce variations to the level using random number generation or other procedural techniques. This could involve adding random obstacles, enemies, or decorative elements.

Example Code (Retrieving Tile Set):

Code snippet

```
// Assuming you have a variable for the selected templateID


dbCommand.CommandText = "SELECT TileSetID FROM LevelTemplates WHERE TemplateID = @templateID";
```

```
dbCommand.Parameters.AddWithValue("@templateID",
templateID);
```

```
int                    tileSetID              =
Convert.ToInt32(dbCommand.ExecuteScalar());
```

```
// Now you can use tileSetID to retrieve the tiles from
the Tiles table
```

Generating Items

You can apply a similar approach to generate items
procedurally. Create tables to store item attributes (e.g.,
name, type, stats, rarity) and use SQL queries to retrieve
these attributes and combine them to create unique
items.

Benefits of Using SQL for Procedural Generation

- **Data-Driven Approach:** Define generation
  parameters and content variations within the
  database, allowing for easy modification and
  updates without altering code.

- **Content Management:** Organize and manage your procedural content in a structured manner, making it easier to create, edit, and reuse assets.
- **Complex Rules and Logic:** Implement complex generation rules and logic using SQL queries and stored procedures.
- **Scalability:** Generate vast amounts of content efficiently by leveraging the power of SQL databases.

Advanced Techniques

- **Weighted Randomization:** Use SQL queries with weighted averages or random functions to generate content with varying probabilities (e.g., rare items have a lower chance of being generated).
- **Constraints and Dependencies:** Implement constraints and dependencies between generated elements to ensure logical consistency (e.g., certain items can only be found in specific environments).
- **Evolutionary Algorithms:** Combine SQL with evolutionary algorithms to generate content that evolves over time or adapts to player behavior.

By integrating SQL with procedural generation, you can create dynamic and engaging game worlds filled with unique content, offering players endless possibilities for exploration and discovery.

Implementing an Online Leaderboard (Storing and retrieving scores, security considerations)

Online leaderboards fuel competition and provide a sense of community in games. They allow players to compare their skills, strive for higher rankings, and celebrate their achievements. This section outlines how to implement an online leaderboard using SQL, covering data storage, retrieval, and crucial security considerations.

Database Design

1. **Players Table:** (This table likely already exists from previous chapters)

Column Name	Data Type	Constraints
PlayerID	INTEGER	PRIMARY KEY
Username	TEXT	NOT NULL, UNIQUE

2. **Leaderboard Table:**

Column Name	Data Type	Constraints
LeaderboardID	INTEGER	PRIMARY KEY
PlayerID	INTEGER	FOREIGN KEY referencing Players table
Score	INTEGER	NOT NULL
Timestamp

DATETIME | NOT NULL | (for tracking when the score was achieved)

This design allows you to store scores associated with individual players and track when those scores were achieved. You can have multiple leaderboards for different game modes or time periods.

Storing Scores

1. **Submit Score:** When a player achieves a score worthy of the leaderboard (e.g., completing a level, winning a match), send the score, PlayerID, and timestamp to the server.
2. **Server-Side Validation:** On the server, validate the submitted score to prevent cheating or data manipulation. This might involve checking for unrealistic values or comparing the score against previous scores from the same player.
3. **Insert Score:** If the score is valid, use an INSERT query to add a new row to the Leaderboard table with the PlayerID, score, and timestamp.
4. **Update Leaderboard:** If the leaderboard has a limited size (e.g., top 100 scores), check if the new score qualifies for a position on the leaderboard. If so, use UPDATE and/or DELETE queries to adjust the rankings accordingly.

Retrieving Scores

1. **Request Leaderboard Data:** When a player views the leaderboard, send a request to the server specifying the desired leaderboard (e.g., by LeaderboardID).
2. **Retrieve Scores:** On the server, use a SELECT query to retrieve the top scores from the Leaderboard table, ordered by score in descending order. You can limit the number of scores retrieved to display only the top rankings.
3. **Send Leaderboard Data:** Send the retrieved scores and associated player information (e.g., usernames) back to the client.
4. **Display Leaderboard:** On the client, display the leaderboard data in a UI element, such as a list or table, showing player rankings and scores.

Security Considerations

- **Secure Data Transmission:** Use HTTPS to encrypt communication between the client and server, protecting score data from interception or tampering.
- **Server-Side Validation:** Thoroughly validate all data received from clients to prevent cheating or data manipulation. Implement server-side checks to ensure that scores are legitimate and consistent with game rules.

- **Prevent SQL Injection:** Use parameterized queries or prepared statements to prevent SQL injection vulnerabilities when interacting with the database.
- **Data Sanitization:** Sanitize any user input before storing it in the database to prevent cross-site scripting (XSS) or other attacks.
- **Rate Limiting:** Implement rate limiting to prevent abuse or denial-of-service attacks by limiting the number of score submissions from a single client within a specific time period.
- **Authentication and Authorization:** If your leaderboard requires user accounts, implement secure authentication and authorization mechanisms to ensure that only legitimate users can submit scores and access leaderboard data.

By following these guidelines and prioritizing security, you can create a robust and fair online leaderboard that fosters healthy competition and enhances the social aspect of your game.

Working with Large Datasets (Optimization techniques: indexing, caching, query optimization)

As your game grows and attracts more players, the amount of data stored in your database will inevitably increase. Handling large datasets efficiently is crucial for maintaining smooth performance and preventing lag or slow loading times. This section explores optimization techniques to ensure your game remains responsive even with massive amounts of data.

Indexing

Indexes are like the index at the back of a book; they help the database quickly locate the data it needs without scanning the entire table. This is especially important for large tables where full table scans can be extremely slow.

- **Types of Indexes:**
  - **Clustered Index:** Organizes the data rows physically on the disk in the order of the index. There can be only one clustered index per table. Choose a column that is frequently used in WHERE clauses and has a wide range of unique values.
  - **Non-Clustered Index:** Creates a separate structure that points to the data rows. You can have multiple non-clustered indexes per table. Useful for columns frequently used in ORDER BY clauses or join conditions.
- **Creating Indexes:**

SQL

-- Create a clustered index on the PlayerID column in the Players table

CREATE CLUSTERED INDEX IX_PlayerID ON Players (PlayerID);

-- Create a non-clustered index on the Score column in the Leaderboard table

CREATE INDEX IX_Score ON Leaderboard (Score DESC);

- **Benefits of Indexing:**
  - Faster data retrieval for queries that use indexed columns.
  - Improved performance for sorting and joining operations.
  - Reduced I/O operations, as the database can locate data more efficiently.

Caching

Caching involves storing frequently accessed data in memory to reduce the need to repeatedly retrieve it from the database. This can significantly improve performance, especially for read-heavy operations.

- **Types of Caching:**

- **Query Caching:** The database server itself can cache the results of frequently executed queries. If the same query is executed again, the server can return the cached result instead of re-executing the query.
- **Application-Level Caching:** You can implement caching within your Unity application using data structures like dictionaries or hash tables. Store frequently accessed data in memory and retrieve it from the cache instead of querying the database.

- **Implementing Caching:**
  - For query caching, consult your database server's documentation for configuration options.
  - For application-level caching, identify data that is frequently accessed and implement caching logic in your C# scripts.

- **Benefits of Caching:**
  - Reduced database load and improved response times.
  - Decreased latency for frequently accessed data.
  - Improved scalability, as the cache can handle a portion of the read requests.

Query Optimization

Optimizing your SQL queries is crucial for efficient data retrieval and processing.

- **Tips for Query Optimization:**
    - **Be Specific:** Avoid SELECT * and specify only the columns you need.
    - **Use WHERE Clauses:** Filter data effectively using WHERE clauses to reduce the number of rows processed.
    - **Optimize Joins:** Use the appropriate join type (inner join, left join, etc.) and ensure that join columns are indexed.
    - **Avoid Calculations in WHERE Clauses:** Calculations on indexed columns can prevent the database from using the index efficiently.
    - **Use LIMIT for Large Datasets:** When retrieving large datasets, use LIMIT to retrieve only the necessary rows, especially for pagination.
    - **Analyze Query Plans:** Use your database server's tools to analyze query execution plans and identify potential bottlenecks.
- **Example of Query Optimization:**

SQL

```sql
-- Inefficient query

SELECT * FROM Players WHERE
YEAR(RegistrationDate) = 2024;


-- Optimized query

SELECT PlayerID, Username FROM Players WHERE
RegistrationDate BETWEEN '2024-01-01' AND
'2024-12-31';
```

Other Optimization Techniques

- **Connection Pooling:** Reuse database connections to reduce the overhead of establishing new connections for each query.
- **Asynchronous Operations:** Execute database operations asynchronously to prevent them from blocking the main thread and causing performance issues.
- **Data Partitioning:** Divide large tables into smaller partitions to improve query performance and manageability.
- **Database Tuning:** Consult your database server's documentation for tuning parameters and

configuration options to optimize performance for your specific needs.

By implementing these optimization techniques, you can ensure that your game handles large datasets efficiently, providing a smooth and responsive experience for your players even as your game world and player base expand.

Security Best Practices (Preventing SQL injection attacks)

Protecting your game and its players from malicious attacks is paramount in today's interconnected world. SQL injection is a common and dangerous attack vector that can compromise your database, steal sensitive information, or even disrupt your entire game. This section delves into security best practices, focusing on preventing SQL injection attacks.

Understanding SQL Injection

SQL injection occurs when attackers exploit vulnerabilities in your code to inject malicious SQL code into your database queries. This can allow them to:

- **Retrieve unauthorized data:** Access sensitive player information, such as usernames, passwords, or payment details.

- **Modify or delete data:** Alter or delete game data, disrupting gameplay or causing irreversible damage.
- **Execute arbitrary commands:** Gain control of the database server, potentially compromising the entire system.

Preventing SQL Injection

1. **Parameterized Queries (Prepared Statements)**

   This is the most effective way to prevent SQL injection. Parameterized queries separate the SQL code from the data being passed to the query. This prevents attackers from injecting malicious code, as the database treats the data as literal values rather than executable code.

   Example:

Code snippet

```
// Vulnerable query (using string concatenation)

string query = "SELECT * FROM Players WHERE Username = '" + username + "' AND Password = '" + password + "'";


// Secure query (using parameterized query)
```

```
string query = "SELECT * FROM Players WHERE
Username = @username AND Password = @password";

dbCommand.CommandText = query;

dbCommand.Parameters.AddWithValue("@username",
username);

dbCommand.Parameters.AddWithValue("@password",
password);
```

2. **Input Validation and Sanitization**

   Validate and sanitize all user input before using it
   in SQL queries. This involves:

   - **Data Type Validation:** Ensure that the
     input matches the expected data type
     (e.g., integer, string, date).
   - **Range Checks:** Check if numeric input
     falls within an acceptable range.
   - **Format Validation:** Validate the format
     of input (e.g., email addresses, dates).
   - **Sanitization:** Remove or escape special
     characters that could be used to construct
     malicious SQL code.

3. **Stored Procedures**

   Stored procedures are pre-compiled SQL code
   stored on the database server. They can help
   prevent SQL injection by:

   - **Encapsulation:** Hiding the underlying
     SQL code from the application.
   - **Access Control:** Restricting access to
     specific database operations.
   - **Parameterization:** Accepting parameters
     that are treated as data, not executable
     code.

4. **Least Privilege Principle**

   Grant database users only the necessary
   privileges to perform their tasks. Avoid using
   accounts with excessive permissions, as this can
   increase the potential damage from an SQL
   injection attack.

5. **Escape User Input (Less Recommended)**

   While less secure than parameterized queries,
   escaping user input can provide a basic level of
   protection. This involves adding escape
   characters (e.g., backslashes) before special
   characters in the input. However, this approach is

prone to errors and can be bypassed in some cases.

6. **Regular Security Audits and Penetration Testing**

   Conduct regular security audits and penetration testing to identify and address[1] potential vulnerabilities in your game and database. This helps you stay ahead of attackers and ensure your security measures are up-to-date.

7. **Stay Informed**

   Keep up-to-date with the latest security best practices and vulnerabilities related to your database system. Regularly update your database software and libraries to patch security holes.

By implementing these security measures and prioritizing data protection, you can create a secure gaming environment that safeguards your players and your game's integrity.

Part 3: Projects

Chapter 7: Project 1: The Endless Dungeon

Project Guidelines: Create a procedurally generated dungeon crawler with enemy stats, item drops, and room layouts stored in a database.

In this project, you'll build a 2D dungeon crawler where players explore randomly generated dungeons, battle enemies, collect items, and level up. The dungeon layout, enemy encounters, and item drops will be driven by data stored in a SQL database.

Database Design

1. **Rooms Table:**

Column Name	Data Type	Constraints
RoomID	INTEGER	PRIMARY KEY
RoomType	TEXT	NOT NULL	(e.g., "Start", "Corridor", "Combat", "Treasure")
Width	INTEGER	NOT NULL
Height	INTEGER	NOT NULL

2. **Enemies Table:**

Column Name	Data Type	Constraints
EnemyID	INTEGER	PRIMARY KEY
EnemyName	TEXT	NOT NULL
Health	INTEGER	NOT NULL
Damage	INTEGER	NOT NULL
ExperienceReward	INTEGER	NOT NULL
ItemDropChance	REAL		(e.g., 0.2 for a 20% chance of dropping an item)

3. **Items Table:**

Column Name	Data Type	Constraints
ItemID	INTEGER	PRIMARY KEY
ItemName	TEXT	NOT NULL
ItemType	TEXT		(e.g., "Weapon", "Armor", "Consumable")
Stats	TEXT		(optional, for storing item attributes as JSON)

Procedural Generation

1. **Dungeon Layout:**
   - Choose a starting room type (e.g., "Start").
   - Generate adjacent rooms based on a set of rules (e.g., maximum room count, room types, connectivity).
   - Store the generated room layout in a data structure (e.g., a graph or a grid).
2. **Populate Rooms:**

- For combat rooms, randomly select enemies from the Enemies table based on the room's difficulty level.
- For treasure rooms, randomly select items from the Items table based on the room's rarity.
- For other room types, populate them with appropriate elements (e.g., traps, puzzles).

3. **Connect Rooms:** Create paths between rooms to form a coherent dungeon layout.

Unity Implementation

1. **Database Connection:** Establish a connection to your database using a library like Mono.Data.Sqlite or MySql.Data.
2. **Retrieve Data:** Use SQL queries to fetch room templates, enemies, and items from the database.
3. **Instantiate Game Objects:** Create game objects for rooms, enemies, and items based on the retrieved data.
4. **Handle Player Interaction:** Implement player movement, combat, and item interaction mechanics.
5. **Save and Load:** Save the player's progress, including their position in the dungeon, inventory, and health, to the database. Load this data when the player starts a new session or returns to the game.

Additional Tips

- **Level Design Patterns:** Consider common dungeon design patterns like the "dungeon crawl" or "hub-and-spoke" layout.
- **Room Variety:** Mix up room types to create a variety of challenges and rewards.
- **Enemy Scaling:** Adjust enemy stats based on the player's level or progress.
- **Item Rarity:** Implement a rarity system to make certain items more valuable and harder to obtain.
- **Dynamic Lighting:** Use lighting effects to create atmosphere and guide the player through the dungeon.
- **Sound Design:** Use sound effects and music to enhance the dungeon experience.

By following these guidelines, you can create a compelling and procedurally generated dungeon crawler that provides endless replayability and challenges for your players.

Step-by-step Implementation: Guidance on database design, Unity scripting, and game logic.

Now that you have the project guidelines, let's dive into the step-by-step implementation of your Endless

Dungeon. This section will provide guidance on database design, Unity scripting, and game logic to help you bring your dungeon crawler to life.

1. Database Design and Population

- **Refine Database Schema:**
  - Start with the database schema provided in the previous section (Rooms, Enemies, Items).
  - Add additional fields as needed (e.g., Description for rooms, Sprite for enemies and items, Rarity for items).
  - Consider adding tables for player data (if you want to save player progress) and other game elements (traps, puzzles).
- **Populate the Database:**
  - Use a tool like DB Browser for SQLite or MySQL Workbench to create your database and populate it with data.
  - Create a variety of room types (start rooms, corridors, combat rooms, treasure rooms, boss rooms).
  - Design diverse enemies with different stats, abilities, and item drop chances.
  - Create a range of items with varying rarities and attributes.

2. Unity Project Setup

- **Create a New Project:** In Unity Hub, create a new 2D project and name it "Endless Dungeon."
- **Import Assets:** Import sprites for your player character, enemies, items, and environment tiles.
- **Set Up Scene:** Create a basic scene with a player character and a camera.
- **Install Database Connector:** Import the necessary database connector library (Mono.Data.Sqlite or MySql.Data) into your project.

3. Unity Scripting

- **Database Manager Script:**
  - Create a C# script named DatabaseManager to handle database interactions.
  - Implement methods for establishing a connection, executing queries, and retrieving data.
  - Include error handling and security measures (parameterized queries).
- **Dungeon Generator Script:**
  - Create a C# script named DungeonGenerator to handle procedural generation.
  - Implement the dungeon generation algorithm:
    - Choose a starting room.

- Generate adjacent rooms based on rules and constraints.
- Populate rooms with enemies and items based on database data.
- Connect rooms to form a navigable dungeon.

- **Room, Enemy, and Item Scripts:**
  - Create C# scripts for rooms, enemies, and items to handle their behavior and interactions.
  - Use data retrieved from the database to set their properties (e.g., enemy stats, item attributes).

- **Player Controller Script:**
  - Create a C# script to handle player input, movement, and combat.
  - Implement collision detection and interaction with enemies and items.

4. Game Logic

- **Room Generation:**
  - In the DungeonGenerator script, implement the logic for generating rooms:
    - Retrieve room templates from the database.
    - Instantiate room prefabs based on the templates.

- ■ Position rooms according to the generated layout.
- **Enemy Spawning:**
  - ○ In the DungeonGenerator or Room script, implement the logic for spawning enemies:
    - ■ Retrieve enemy data from the database.
    - ■ Instantiate enemy prefabs based on the data.
    - ■ Position enemies within the room.
- **Item Placement:**
  - ○ In the DungeonGenerator or Room script, implement the logic for placing items:
    - ■ Retrieve item data from the database.
    - ■ Instantiate item prefabs based on the data.
    - ■ Position items within the room.
- **Player Interaction:**
  - ○ In the PlayerController script, implement the logic for player movement, combat, and item collection.
  - ○ Use raycasting or collision detection to detect interactions with enemies and items.
  - ○ Update player stats and inventory based on interactions.

- **Game Over:** Implement game over conditions (e.g., player health reaches zero).

5. Testing and Refinement

- **Test Thoroughly:** Playtest your game extensively to identify bugs, balance issues, and areas for improvement.
- **Refine Gameplay:** Adjust enemy stats, item attributes, and dungeon generation rules to create a balanced and engaging experience.
- **Add Features:** Consider adding additional features like traps, puzzles, boss battles, or a skill tree.
- **Polish Visuals and Sound:** Enhance the game's visuals and sound design to create a more immersive experience.

By following these steps and iteratively refining your game, you can create a compelling and procedurally generated dungeon crawler that provides endless hours of gameplay. Remember to leverage the power of SQL to manage your game data and drive dynamic content creation.

Chapter 8: Project 2: The Online RPG

Project Guidelines: Build a multiplayer game with player accounts, persistent inventory, and a shared world.

This project challenges you to create a 2D online RPG where players can create accounts, interact with each other in a shared world, embark on quests, and manage persistent inventories. This ambitious endeavor will solidify your understanding of SQL integration with Unity, online interactions, and data-driven game development.

Core Features

- **Player Accounts:**
  - Account creation and login using a secure authentication system.
  - Storage of player data (username, password, character information, progress) in a database.
- **Persistent Inventory:**
  - A persistent inventory system that saves and loads player items and equipment to and from the database.
  - Ability to trade items with other players.
- **Shared World:**

- A shared online world where multiple players can interact simultaneously.
  - Synchronization of player positions, actions, and world state.
- **Quests:**
  - A quest system with objectives, rewards, and progress tracking stored in the database.
  - Ability to complete quests solo or with other players.
- **Combat:**
  - Real-time combat system with player vs. enemy and player vs. player (PvP) interactions.
  - Synchronization of combat actions and effects across the network.

Database Design

1. **Accounts Table:**

Column Name	Data Type	Constraints
AccountID	INTEGER	PRIMARY KEY
Username	TEXT	NOT NULL, UNIQUE
PasswordHash	TEXT	NOT NULL (store hashed passwords for security)

2. **Players Table:**

Column Name	Data Type	Constraints
PlayerID	INTEGER	PRIMARY KEY
AccountID	INTEGER	FOREIGN KEY referencing Accounts table
CharacterName	TEXT	NOT NULL
Level	INTEGER	NOT NULL
Experience	INTEGER	NOT NULL
PositionX	REAL	
PositionY	REAL	

3. **Inventory Table:**

Column Name	Data Type	Constraints
InventoryID	INTEGER	PRIMARY KEY
PlayerID	INTEGER	FOREIGN KEY referencing Players table
ItemID	INTEGER	FOREIGN KEY referencing Items table
Quantity	INTEGER	NOT NULL, CHECK (Quantity >= 0)

4. **Quests Table:** (Similar to the structure in Chapter 5)

Column Name	Data Type	Constraints
QuestID	INTEGER	PRIMARY KEY
QuestName	TEXT	NOT NULL
Description	TEXT	
RewardXP	INTEGER	
RewardItemID	INTEGER	FOREIGN KEY referencing Items table

5. **Objectives Table:** (Similar to the structure in Chapter 5)

Column Name	Data Type	Constraints
ObjectiveID	INTEGER	PRIMARY KEY
QuestID	INTEGER	FOREIGN KEY referencing Quests table
Description	TEXT	NOT NULL
TargetAmount	INTEGER	
CurrentAmount	INTEGER	

6. **PlayerQuests Table:** (Similar to the structure in Chapter 5)

Column Name	Data Type	Constraints
PlayerQuestID	INTEGER	PRIMARY KEY
PlayerID	INTEGER	FOREIGN KEY referencing Players table
QuestID	INTEGER	FOREIGN KEY referencing Quests table
Status	TEXT	
CurrentObjectiveID	INTEGER	FOREIGN KEY referencing Objectives table

Implementation Considerations

- **Networking:**
  - Choose a networking solution (e.g., Unity's built-in networking, Mirror, Photon) to handle communication between clients and the server.

- Implement client-side prediction and server reconciliation to ensure smooth and responsive gameplay.
- Handle network latency and potential packet loss.

- **Server-Side Logic:**
  - Implement server-side logic to handle player authentication, data validation, and world state synchronization.
  - Use a server-authoritative approach to prevent cheating and ensure data integrity.

- **Client-Side Logic:**
  - Implement client-side logic to handle player input, rendering, and user interface.
  - Optimize client-side performance to ensure smooth gameplay.

- **Security:**
  - Implement secure authentication and authorization to protect player accounts.
  - Use parameterized queries to prevent SQL injection attacks.
  - Validate and sanitize all user input.

Additional Features (Optional)

- **Chat System:** Allow players to communicate with each other in the game world.

- **Guilds or Clans:** Implement social features for players to form groups and collaborate.
- **Trading System:** Enable players to trade items with each other.
- **Crafting System:** Allow players to craft new items using resources.
- **PvP Zones:** Designate areas for player vs. player combat.

By successfully completing this project, you'll gain valuable experience in building online multiplayer games with persistent data and dynamic interactions, showcasing your mastery of SQL and Unity for data-driven game development.

Step-by-step Implementation: Focus on online database interactions, user authentication, and data synchronization.

Building an online RPG involves intricate interactions between clients and the server, secure authentication for player accounts, and seamless data synchronization to maintain a consistent game world. This section provides a step-by-step guide with a focus on these crucial aspects.

1. Choose a Networking Solution

- Select a networking solution that suits your needs and project scope. Popular options include:
    - **Unity's built-in networking:** Provides a basic framework for networking but may require more manual implementation.
    - **Mirror:** A user-friendly and feature-rich networking library for Unity.
    - **Photon:** A robust and scalable networking solution with a focus on multiplayer games.

2. Server Setup

- Set up a dedicated server or use a cloud-based solution to host your game server.
- Install the necessary server-side components for your chosen networking solution.
- Ensure your server has sufficient resources (CPU, memory, bandwidth) to handle multiple players.

3. Database Connection (Server-Side)

- In your server-side scripts, establish a connection to your SQL database using the appropriate connector library (Mono.Data.Sqlite or MySql.Data).
- Implement security measures to protect the database connection and prevent unauthorized access.

4. User Authentication

- **Account Creation:**
  - When a player creates an account, receive their username and password from the client.
  - Hash the password using a strong hashing algorithm (e.g., bcrypt, scrypt) before storing it in the Accounts table.
  - Generate a unique AccountID and store it along with the hashed password and username.
- **Login:**
  - When a player logs in, receive their username and password from the client.
  - Retrieve the stored password hash from the Accounts table based on the username.
  - Compare the submitted password with the stored hash using the same hashing algorithm.
  - If the hashes match, authenticate the user and generate a session token or ID to maintain their login state.
- **Security:**
  - Use HTTPS to encrypt communication between the client and server during authentication.

- Implement measures to prevent brute-force attacks (e.g., account lockouts, CAPTCHAs).
- Consider using two-factor authentication for added security.

5. Data Synchronization

- **Player Position and Actions:**
    - Continuously send player position and action updates from the client to the server.
    - Validate and process these updates on the server to ensure consistency and prevent cheating.
    - Broadcast the validated updates to other clients in the shared world.
- **World State:**
    - Synchronize changes to the world state (e.g., enemy positions, item spawns, quest progress) between the server and clients.
    - Use techniques like delta compression or state synchronization to minimize the amount of data transmitted.
- **Inventory:**
    - When a player acquires or uses an item, update the Inventory table on the server.

- Synchronize the inventory changes with the client to reflect the updated inventory state.
- **Quests:**
  - When a player accepts or completes a quest or objective, update the PlayerQuests and Objectives tables on the server.
  - Synchronize the quest progress with the client to update the quest log.

6. Client-Side Implementation

- **Connect to Server:** Implement client-side logic to connect to the game server using the chosen networking solution.
- **Handle User Input:** Capture player input and send it to the server for processing.
- **Render Game World:** Receive world state updates from the server and render the game world accordingly.
- **Display UI:** Display player information, inventory, quest log, and other UI elements based on synchronized data.

7. Testing and Refinement

- **Test with Multiple Players:** Thoroughly test your game with multiple players to identify and address any networking or synchronization issues.

- **Optimize Performance:** Optimize both server-side and client-side code to ensure smooth performance and minimize latency.
- **Refine Gameplay:** Balance gameplay mechanics, adjust difficulty, and fine-tune interactions based on player feedback.

By carefully implementing online database interactions, user authentication, and data synchronization, you can create an engaging and immersive online RPG experience for your players. Remember to prioritize security and performance to ensure a smooth and enjoyable gameplay experience.

Part 4: Going Further

Chapter 9: Beyond the Basics

Advanced SQL Queries (Subqueries, aggregate functions, views)

As you delve deeper into the world of SQL and data-driven game development, mastering advanced query techniques becomes essential. This chapter explores powerful tools like subqueries, aggregate functions, and views, empowering you to perform complex data manipulation and analysis, ultimately leading to richer and more dynamic game experiences.

Subqueries

Subqueries, also known as nested queries, are queries embedded within another SQL query. They allow you to perform multi-step operations, retrieve data based on dynamic conditions, and create more sophisticated logic within your SQL statements.

- **Types of Subqueries:**
  - **Scalar Subqueries:** Return a single value. Often used to retrieve aggregate values or perform comparisons.

```sql
SELECT ItemName FROM Items WHERE Price =
(SELECT MAX(Price) FROM Items);
```

-- Retrieves the name of the most expensive item.

- o **Multi-row Subqueries:** Return multiple rows. Used with operators like IN, ANY, or ALL to compare values against a set of results.

SQL

```sql
SELECT PlayerID, Username FROM Players WHERE
PlayerID IN (SELECT PlayerID FROM PlayerQuests
WHERE QuestID = 1);
```

-- Retrieves players who have accepted quest with ID 1.

- Correlated Subqueries: Reference columns from the outer query. Executed once for each row in the outer query.

SQL

```
SELECT PlayerID, Username FROM Players p WHERE
EXISTS (SELECT 1 FROM Inventory i WHERE
i.PlayerID = p.PlayerID AND i.ItemID = 5);
```

-- Retrieves players who have item with ID 5 in their inventory.

- **Benefits of Subqueries:**
  - **Modularization:** Break down complex queries into smaller, more manageable components.
  - **Dynamic Filtering:** Filter data based on the results of another query.
  - **Code Reusability:** Reuse subqueries in multiple parts of a larger query.

Aggregate Functions

Aggregate functions perform calculations on a set of values and return a single value. They are essential for summarizing data, calculating statistics, and gaining insights from your database.

- **Common Aggregate Functions:**
  - AVG(): Calculates the average value of a column.
  - COUNT(): Counts the number of rows or non-null values.
  - MAX(): Returns the maximum value in a column.
  - MIN(): Returns the minimum value in a column.
  - SUM(): Calculates the sum of values in a column.[1]
- **Example:**

SQL

SELECT AVG(Score) AS AverageScore, MAX(Score) AS HighScore FROM Leaderboard;

-- Retrieves the average and highest score from the Leaderboard table.

- **Using Aggregate Functions with** GROUP BY:
- The GROUP BY clause groups rows with the same values in one or more columns. This allows you to apply aggregate functions to each group.

SQL

```
SELECT PlayerID, COUNT(QuestID) AS CompletedQuests FROM PlayerQuests WHERE Status = 'Completed' GROUP BY PlayerID;
```

-- Retrieves the number of completed quests for each player.

Views

Views are virtual tables based on the result-set of an SQL statement. They provide a way to simplify complex queries, enhance data security, and customize data presentation.

- **Creating a View:**

SQL

```sql
CREATE VIEW ActivePlayers AS

SELECT PlayerID, Username, Level FROM Players
WHERE LastLoginDate >= DATE('now', '-7 days');
```

-- Creates a view named "ActivePlayers" that shows players who logged in within the last 7 days.

- **Using a View:**

SQL

```sql
SELECT * FROM ActivePlayers WHERE Level > 10;
```

-- Retrieves active players with a level greater than 10.

- **Benefits of Views:**
  - **Simplified Queries:** Hide complex logic behind a simple view name.

- o **Data Security:** Restrict access to specific columns or rows through views.
- o **Data Integrity:** Enforce data consistency by providing a controlled view of the data.
- o **Code Maintainability:** Changes to the underlying tables are automatically reflected in the view.

By mastering these advanced SQL techniques, you can unlock the full potential of your database and create more dynamic, data-driven game experiences. Subqueries enable complex logic, aggregate functions provide valuable insights, and views simplify data access and management.

Database Administration (Backups, security, performance monitoring)

While mastering SQL queries is essential, understanding database administration is crucial for long-term success in data-driven game development. This section delves into key aspects of database administration, including backups, security measures beyond preventing SQL injection, and performance monitoring to ensure your database remains robust, secure, and optimized.

Backups: Safeguarding Your Precious Data

Regular backups are your insurance policy against data loss due to hardware failures, software errors, or malicious attacks. They ensure that you can restore your game data to a previous state in case of unexpected events.

- **Backup Strategies:**
  - **Full Backups:** Create a complete copy of the entire database.
  - **Incremental Backups:** Back up only the changes made since the last full or incremental backup.
  - **Differential Backups:** Back up only the changes made since the last full backup.
- **Backup Frequency:**
  - Determine the appropriate backup frequency based on the rate of data change and your risk tolerance.
  - For games with frequent updates or online interactions, consider daily or even hourly backups.
- **Backup Storage:**
  - Store backups in a secure, off-site location to protect against physical damage or theft.
  - Consider cloud-based backup solutions for added redundancy and accessibility.
- **Backup Restoration:**

- Regularly test your backup restoration process to ensure that you can recover data effectively in case of an emergency.
- Document the restoration process clearly for easy reference.

Security: A Multi-Layered Approach

Database security extends beyond preventing SQL injection. It involves a multi-layered approach to protect your data from unauthorized access, modification, or deletion.

- **Access Control:**
  - Implement strong authentication and authorization mechanisms to restrict access to your database.
  - Use role-based access control (RBAC) to assign permissions to different users or groups based on their roles and responsibilities.
- **Encryption:**
  - Encrypt sensitive data both in transit (using SSL/TLS) and at rest (using database encryption).
  - This adds an extra layer of protection against unauthorized access even if the database is compromised.
- **Auditing:**

- Enable database auditing to track user activity and identify suspicious behavior.
- Regularly review audit logs to detect potential security breaches or unauthorized access attempts.
- **Firewall:**
  - Use a firewall to restrict access to your database server from unauthorized IP addresses or networks.
  - Configure the firewall to allow only necessary connections on specific ports.
- **Regular Security Assessments:**
  - Conduct regular security assessments and penetration testing to identify and address potential[1] vulnerabilities.
  - Stay informed about the latest security threats and vulnerabilities related to your database system.

Performance Monitoring

Monitoring database performance is crucial for identifying bottlenecks, optimizing queries, and ensuring a smooth gaming experience.

- **Key Performance Indicators (KPIs):**
  - **Query response time:** Measure the time it takes for queries to execute.

- ○ **CPU usage:** Monitor the CPU load on the database server.
  - ○ **Memory usage:** Track memory consumption by the database server.
  - ○ **Disk I/O:** Measure the rate of data read and write operations.
  - ○ **Network traffic:** Monitor the network bandwidth used by the database server.
- **Monitoring Tools:**
  - ○ Use database monitoring tools or built-in server features to track KPIs and identify performance issues.
  - ○ Set up alerts and notifications to be informed of critical events or performance thresholds.
- **Performance Optimization:**
  - ○ Analyze query performance using profiling tools to identify slow or inefficient queries.
  - ○ Optimize database schema, indexes, and queries to improve performance.
  - ○ Consider using caching or data partitioning to enhance scalability and reduce database load.

By diligently implementing these database administration practices, you can ensure that your database remains a reliable, secure, and high-performing foundation for your data-driven game. Regular backups protect against data loss, robust security measures safeguard against attacks, and performance monitoring helps optimize the gaming experience for your players.

Alternative Database Solutions (NoSQL databases, cloud databases)

While relational databases like SQLite and MySQL are excellent choices for many game development projects, exploring alternative database solutions can open up new possibilities and address specific needs. This section delves into two prominent alternatives: NoSQL databases and cloud databases.

NoSQL Databases

NoSQL databases offer a departure from the traditional relational model, providing flexible schemas and specialized features for handling diverse data types and large-scale applications.

- **Types of NoSQL Databases:**
  - **Document Databases:** Store data in flexible, semi-structured documents (e.g., JSON, XML). Suitable for content management, user profiles, and dynamic game content. (e.g., MongoDB)

- **Key-Value Stores:** Store data as key-value pairs. Excellent for caching, session management, and storing player preferences. (e.g., Redis)
- **Graph Databases:** Represent data as nodes and relationships. Ideal for social networks, recommendation systems, and in-game relationships. (e.g., Neo4j)
- **Wide-Column Stores:** Store data in columns instead of rows. Efficient for large datasets and analytical queries. (e.g., Cassandra)

- **Benefits of NoSQL Databases:**
  - **Schema Flexibility:** Adapt to changing data structures without complex migrations.
  - **Scalability:** Handle large volumes of data and high traffic loads.
  - **Specialized Features:** Offer features tailored to specific data types and use cases.
  - **Performance:** Can provide high performance for specific types of queries and operations.

- **Considerations for Game Development:**
  - **Data Model:** Choose a NoSQL model that aligns with your game's data structure and access patterns.

- **Consistency:** Understand the consistency guarantees of the chosen NoSQL database (e.g., eventual consistency vs. strong consistency).
- **Query Language:** Learn the query language specific to the NoSQL database (e.g., MongoDB's query language, Redis commands).
- **Integration:** Explore libraries and tools for integrating the NoSQL database with Unity.

Cloud Databases

Cloud databases offer a managed solution for hosting and managing your database in the cloud. They provide scalability, reliability, and reduced administrative overhead.

- **Popular Cloud Database Providers:**
  - **AWS:** Amazon Relational Database Service (RDS), Amazon Aurora, Amazon DynamoDB
  - **Google Cloud:** Cloud SQL, Cloud Spanner, Cloud Firestore
  - **Microsoft Azure:** Azure SQL Database, Azure Cosmos DB
- **Benefits of Cloud Databases:**

- Scalability: Easily scale your database resources (CPU, memory, storage) as needed.
- Reliability: High availability and fault tolerance with automatic backups and failover mechanisms.
- Managed Services: Reduced administrative overhead with automated patching, updates, and security management.
- Cost-Effectiveness: Pay-as-you-go pricing models can be more cost-effective than managing your own infrastructure.

- **Considerations for Game Development:**
  - Latency: Consider the latency between your game servers and the cloud database.
  - Cost: Evaluate pricing models and potential costs associated with data storage, transfer, and usage.
  - Vendor Lock-In: Be aware of potential vendor lock-in when choosing a cloud provider.
  - Security: Understand the security measures and compliance certifications offered by the cloud provider.

Choosing the Right Solution

The choice between relational, NoSQL, or cloud databases depends on your game's specific needs and priorities.

- **Relational Databases:** Excellent for structured data, complex relationships, and ACID properties (Atomicity, Consistency, Isolation, Durability).
- **NoSQL Databases:** Suitable for flexible schemas, large datasets, and specialized use cases.
- **Cloud Databases:** Offer scalability, reliability, and managed services with potential cost benefits.

Consider factors like data structure, scalability requirements, performance needs, security concerns, and budget constraints when making your decision.

Chapter 10: Resources and Community

Useful Online Resources (SQL documentation, Unity forums, game development communities)

The journey of learning and mastering SQL for Unity game development is an ongoing one. Thankfully, a wealth of online resources exists to support you, provide answers, and connect you with a vibrant community of fellow developers. This section highlights some of the most valuable resources to fuel your growth and keep you at the forefront of data-driven game development.

SQL Documentation and Learning Platforms

- **Official SQL Documentation:**
    - **MySQL:** dev.mysql.com/doc/]([invalid URL removed]) - Comprehensive documentation for MySQL, covering everything from basic syntax to advanced features.
    - **SQLite:** [www.sqlite.org/docs.html [invalid URL removed] - Official documentation for SQLite, including tutorials, command references, and language specifications.

- **W3Schools SQL Tutorial:** www.w3schools.com/sql/]([invalid URL removed]) - A beginner-friendly and interactive tutorial for learning SQL fundamentals.
- **Khan Academy SQL Course:** [www.khanacademy.org/computing/computer-programming/sql [invalid URL removed] - A free and structured course covering the basics of SQL and database concepts.
- **SQLZoo:** sqlzoo.net]([invalid URL removed]) - An interactive platform with tutorials and exercises for practicing SQL queries on various databases.

Unity Forums and Communities

- **Unity Forum:** [forum.unity.com [invalid URL removed] - The official Unity forum, a hub for discussions, questions, and support related to all aspects of Unity development, including database integration.
- **Unity Answers:** answers.unity.com [invalid URL removed] - A Q&A platform where you can ask questions and find solutions to common Unity development challenges.
- **Unity Discord Server:** [invalid URL removed] - A vibrant Discord community where Unity

developers connect, share knowledge, and collaborate.

- **Reddit r/Unity3D:** www.reddit.com/r/Unity3D/]([invalid URL removed]) - A subreddit dedicated to Unity development, with discussions, tutorials, and news.

Game Development Communities

- **GameDev.net:** [www.gamedev.net] - A long-standing community for game developers, offering forums, articles, and resources on various aspects of game development.
- **GDC Vault:** www.gdcvault.com - A collection of talks and presentations from the Game Developers Conference (GDC), providing insights from industry professionals.
- **TIGSource:** [www.tigsource.com- A community focused on independent game development, with forums, articles, and showcases of indie games.

Specialized Resources

- **GitHub:** github.com]([invalid URL removed]) - Explore open-source projects, libraries, and code examples related to SQL and Unity integration.
- **Stack Overflow:** [stackoverflow.com [invalid URL removed] - A Q&A platform for programmers, where you can find solutions to

specific coding challenges and database-related questions.

Tips for Utilizing Online Resources

- **Be Specific:** When asking questions, provide clear and concise descriptions of your problem, including code snippets and error messages.
- **Search Before Asking:** Search forums and documentation for existing solutions before posting a new question.
- **Engage with the Community:** Participate in discussions, offer help to others, and contribute to the community's knowledge base.
- **Stay Updated:** Follow blogs, newsletters, and social media accounts of Unity and SQL experts to stay informed about the latest trends and techniques.

By actively engaging with these online resources and the wider game development community, you can accelerate your learning, overcome challenges, and unlock the full potential of SQL and Unity for creating innovative and data-driven games.

Troubleshooting and Debugging Tips

Even with the best resources and careful planning, encountering challenges and bugs in your SQL and Unity projects is inevitable. This section equips you with essential troubleshooting and debugging tips to overcome these hurdles and emerge as a more resilient and resourceful developer.

General Troubleshooting Strategies

- **Isolate the Problem:** Break down the issue into smaller, more manageable parts. Identify whether the problem originates in your SQL code, Unity scripts, or the interaction between them.
- **Check for Obvious Errors:** Review your code for syntax errors, typos, incorrect database credentials, or missing libraries. These simple oversights can often cause significant problems.
- **Test with Simple Cases:** Start with a simplified version of your code or database structure to isolate the core issue. Gradually add complexity to pinpoint the source of the problem.
- **Read Error Messages Carefully:** Pay close attention to error messages in Unity's console and your database server's logs. They often provide valuable clues about the nature and location of the error.
- **Consult the Documentation:** Refer to the official documentation for Unity, your database system, and any libraries you're using. They often contain troubleshooting sections and solutions to common problems.

- **Google is Your Friend:** Don't hesitate to search online for solutions to your specific error messages or challenges. Many developers have likely encountered and solved similar problems.

Debugging Techniques

- **Unity Debugger:**
  - Use Unity's built-in debugger to step through your C# code line by line, inspect variables, and set breakpoints to pause execution at specific points.
  - This allows you to observe the flow of your code and identify where errors occur.
- **Database Debugging Tools:**
  - Explore debugging tools provided by your database system (e.g., MySQL Workbench's debugger) to step through SQL queries, examine query plans, and identify performance bottlenecks.
- **Logging:**
  - Add Debug.Log statements to your Unity scripts to track the execution flow and values of variables.
  - Use logging features in your database server to record queries, errors, and performance metrics.
- **Testing:**

- Write unit tests for your C# scripts and SQL queries to ensure they function correctly in isolation.
- Implement integration tests to verify the interaction between your Unity code and the database.

Specific Troubleshooting Scenarios

- **Connection Errors:**
  - Double-check your connection string for accuracy, including database path, server address, username, and password.
  - Ensure that the database server is running and accessible.
  - Verify that your firewall is not blocking database connections.

- **Query Errors:**
  - Review your SQL queries for syntax errors or incorrect table or column names.
  - Use parameterized queries to prevent SQL injection vulnerabilities.
  - Analyze query plans to identify performance bottlenecks.

- **Data Inconsistencies:**
  - Implement data validation and sanitization to ensure data integrity.
  - Use database constraints to enforce data rules and relationships.

- Check for data redundancy or inconsistencies that could lead to unexpected behavior.
- **Performance Issues:**
  - Use indexing and caching to optimize data retrieval.
  - Optimize queries to reduce database load and improve response times.
  - Monitor database performance to identify bottlenecks and areas for improvement.

Seeking Help

- **Online Communities:** Don't hesitate to ask for help in online forums, communities, or Q&A platforms like Stack Overflow.
- **Collaborate with Others:** Pair programming or code reviews with fellow developers can provide fresh perspectives and identify issues you might have missed.
- **Seek Expert Advice:** If you're facing complex challenges, consider seeking guidance from experienced SQL or Unity developers.

By mastering these troubleshooting and debugging techniques, you'll be well-equipped to tackle challenges, resolve errors, and create robust and reliable data-driven games. Remember that debugging is an essential part of the development process, and each challenge you overcome makes you a stronger and more capable developer.

Next Steps in Your Game Development Journey

Congratulations! You've reached the end of this journey into the world of SQL and Unity for 2D game development. But this is just the beginning of your exciting adventure as a data-driven game developer. This section outlines some paths you can explore to further enhance your skills, expand your knowledge, and create even more compelling and innovative games.

1. Deepen Your SQL Expertise

- **Advanced SQL Concepts:** Dive deeper into advanced SQL topics like stored procedures, triggers, transactions, and database optimization techniques.
- **Database Administration:** Learn about database administration, including backup and recovery, security management, and performance tuning.
- **Explore Different Database Systems:** Experiment with other relational databases (PostgreSQL, Oracle) or NoSQL databases (MongoDB, Redis) to broaden your

understanding and choose the best solution for different projects.

2. Expand Your Unity Skills

- **Advanced Unity Features:** Master advanced Unity features like shaders, particle systems, animation systems, and AI for more sophisticated game mechanics and visuals.
- **Game Design Patterns:** Study common game design patterns and architectural patterns to create well-structured and maintainable game code.
- **Performance Optimization:** Learn advanced performance optimization techniques for Unity, including profiling, memory management, and rendering optimization.

3. Explore Specialized Areas

- **Multiplayer Game Development:** Delve deeper into online multiplayer game development, including networking, server architecture, and client-server communication.
- **Procedural Content Generation:** Master advanced procedural generation techniques to create vast and dynamic game worlds.
- **Data Analytics for Games:** Learn how to collect and analyze player data to gain insights into player behavior, improve game design, and make data-driven decisions.

- **Game AI:** Explore the world of game AI, including pathfinding, decision-making, and machine learning for more intelligent and engaging game characters.

4. Build a Portfolio

- **Personal Projects:** Create your own game projects to apply your skills, experiment with new ideas, and build a portfolio of your work.
- **Game Jams:** Participate in game jams to challenge yourself, collaborate with others, and gain experience in rapid game development.
- **Contribute to Open-Source Projects:** Contribute to open-source game projects to learn from experienced developers and gain real-world experience.

5. Connect with the Community

- **Attend Game Development Events:** Attend conferences, workshops, and meetups to network with other developers, learn from industry experts, and stay updated on the latest trends.
- **Join Online Communities:** Participate in online forums, communities, and social media groups to connect with fellow developers, share knowledge, and find support.

6. Never Stop Learning

- **Stay Curious:** Continuously explore new technologies, game development techniques, and SQL advancements to stay at the forefront of the industry.
- **Embrace Challenges:** Don't be afraid to tackle challenging projects and push your skills to the limit.
- **Share Your Knowledge:** Teach and mentor others to solidify your understanding and contribute to the growth of the game development community.

By following these next steps and maintaining a passion for learning and creating, you can embark on a fulfilling and successful journey as a SQL-savvy Unity game developer, bringing your innovative and data-driven game ideas to life.

Appendices

Appendix A: SQL Cheat Sheet

This cheat sheet provides a quick reference for essential SQL commands and concepts covered throughout this book. It's a handy resource to refresh your memory and have key syntax at your fingertips as you develop your SQL skills for Unity game development.

Basic Commands

Command	Description	Example
SELECT	Retrieves data from a table.	SELECT * FROM Players;
WHERE	Filters data based on a condition.	SELECT * FROM Items WHERE Price < 50;
ORDER BY	Sorts data based on one or more columns.	SELECT * FROM Players ORDER BY Score DESC;
INSERT INTO	Inserts new data into a table.	INSERT INTO Players (Username, Level) VALUES ('NewPlayer', 1);

| UPDATE | Updates existing data in a table. | UPDATE Players SET Level = 2 WHERE PlayerID = 1; |
| DELETE | Deletes data from a table. | DELETE FROM Players WHERE PlayerID = 1; |

Data Types

Data Type	Description
INTEGER	Whole numbers
REAL	Decimal numbers
TEXT	Strings of characters
BLOB	Binary data
BOOLEAN	True/false values
DATE	Dates
TIME	Time

Constraints

Constraint	Description
NOT NULL	Ensures a column cannot contain a null value.
UNIQUE	Ensures all values in a column are unique.
PRIMARY KEY	Uniquely identifies each row in a table.
FOREIGN KEY	Establishes a relationship between tables.
CHECK	Ensures a value meets a specific condition.

Operators

Operator	Description
=	Equal to
!= or <>	Not equal to
>	Greater than
<	Less than

>=	Greater than or equal to
<=	Less than or equal to
AND	Combines conditions where both must be true.
OR	Combines conditions where at least one must be true.
NOT	Negates a condition.
LIKE	Matches patterns in text data
BETWEEN	Checks if a value is within a range.
IN	Checks if a value is in a list of values.

Aggregate Functions

Function	Description
AVG()	Calculates the average value.
COUNT()	Counts the number of rows or values.

MAX()	Returns the maximum value.
MIN()	Returns the minimum value.
SUM()	Calculates the sum of values.

Joins

Join Type	Description
INNER JOIN	Returns rows where the join condition is met in both tables.
LEFT JOIN	Returns all rows from the left table and matching rows from the right table.
RIGHT JOIN	Returns all rows from the right table and matching rows from the left table.
FULL OUTER JOIN	Returns all rows[1] from both tables, regardless of whether there is a match.

Subqueries

- Queries nested within another query.

- Can be used for dynamic filtering, multi-step operations, and complex logic.

Views

- Virtual tables based on the result-set of an SQL statement.
- Simplify complex queries, enhance data security, and customize data presentation.

Tips

- Use descriptive names for tables and columns.
- Choose appropriate data types for each column.
- Enforce data integrity with constraints.
- Optimize queries for performance.
- Use parameterized queries to prevent SQL injection.
- Back up your database regularly.

This cheat sheet provides a condensed overview of essential SQL elements. Remember to refer to the relevant chapters in the book for detailed explanations, examples, and best practices.

Appendix B: C# Scripting Examples

This appendix provides a collection of C# scripting examples demonstrating key concepts and techniques for interacting with SQL databases in Unity. These examples can serve as a starting point for your own code and inspire you to explore further possibilities.

1. Connecting to an SQLite Database

Code snippet

```csharp
using UnityEngine;
using Mono.Data.Sqlite;
using System.Data;


public class SQLiteConnectionExample : MonoBehaviour
{
    void Start()
    {
        string connectionString = "URI=file:" + Application.dataPath + "/MyDatabase.db";


        try
```

```
        {
                using (IDbConnection dbConnection = new
SqliteConnection(connectionString))
            {
            dbConnection.Open();

            Debug.Log("Connected to SQLite database!");

            dbConnection.Close();

            }

        }

    catch (Exception ex)

        {

            Debug.LogError("Database connection error: " +
ex.Message);

            }

        }

}
```

2. Connecting to a MySQL Database

Code snippet

```
using UnityEngine;
```

```csharp
using MySql.Data.MySqlClient;
using System.Data;

public class MySQLConnectionExample : MonoBehaviour
{
    void Start()
    {
        string connectionString = "Server=localhost;Database=mydatabase;User ID=your_username;Password=your_password;";

        try
        {
            using (IDbConnection dbConnection = new MySqlConnection(connectionString))
            {
                dbConnection.Open();
                Debug.Log("Connected to MySQL database!");
                dbConnection.Close();
            }
```

```
        }
    catch (Exception ex)
        {
            Debug.LogError("Database connection error: " +
ex.Message);
        }
    }
}
```

3. Executing a SELECT Query

Code snippet

```
// ... (connection establishment code) ...


IDbCommand           dbCommand           =
dbConnection.CreateCommand();
dbCommand.CommandText   =   "SELECT   PlayerID,
Username FROM Players WHERE Level > 5";


IDataReader reader = dbCommand.ExecuteReader();
```

```csharp
while (reader.Read())
{
    int playerID = reader.GetInt32(0);
    string username = reader.GetString(1);
    Debug.Log("Player ID: " + playerID + ", Username: "
+ username);
}


reader.Close();
// ... (connection closing code) ...
```

4. Executing an INSERT Query

Code snippet

```csharp
// ... (connection establishment code) ...


IDbCommand             dbCommand             =
dbConnection.CreateCommand();
dbCommand.CommandText = "INSERT INTO Players
(Username, Level) VALUES (@username, @level)";
```

```csharp
dbCommand.Parameters.AddWithValue("@username",
"NewPlayer");

dbCommand.Parameters.AddWithValue("@level", 1);


int rowsAffected = dbCommand.ExecuteNonQuery();


if (rowsAffected > 0)
{

    Debug.Log("Player inserted successfully!");

}


// ... (connection closing code) ...
```

5. Executing an UPDATE Query

Code snippet

```csharp
// ... (connection establishment code) ...


IDbCommand                    dbCommand                    =
dbConnection.CreateCommand();
```

```csharp
dbCommand.CommandText = "UPDATE Players SET
Level = @level WHERE PlayerID = @playerID";

dbCommand.Parameters.AddWithValue("@level", 10);

dbCommand.Parameters.AddWithValue("@playerID",
1);


int rowsAffected = dbCommand.ExecuteNonQuery();


if (rowsAffected > 0)
{
    Debug.Log("Player level updated successfully!");
}


// ... (connection closing code) ...
```

6. Executing a DELETE Query

Code snippet

```csharp
// ... (connection establishment code) ...
```

```
IDbCommand               dbCommand         =
dbConnection.CreateCommand();

dbCommand.CommandText = "DELETE FROM Players
WHERE PlayerID = @playerID";

dbCommand.Parameters.AddWithValue("@playerID",
1);


int rowsAffected = dbCommand.ExecuteNonQuery();


if (rowsAffected > 0)
{
    Debug.Log("Player deleted successfully!");
}


// ... (connection closing code) ...
```

7. Serializing Data with JSON

Code snippet

```
// Assuming you have a Player class with properties for
player data
```

```
Player player = new Player();

// ... populate the player object with data ...


string jsonData = JsonUtility.ToJson(player);


// ... use an INSERT or UPDATE query to store jsonData
in the database ...
```

8. Deserializing Data with JSON

Code snippet

```
// ... retrieve jsonData from the database using a
SELECT query ...


Player player =
JsonUtility.FromJson<Player>(jsonData);


// ... use the deserialized data to update the game state ...
```

These examples provide a foundation for interacting with SQL databases in Unity. Remember to adapt and expand upon these examples to suit your specific game development needs. Refer to the relevant chapters for more detailed explanations and advanced techniques.

Appendix C: Database Design Best Practices

Designing an effective and efficient database is crucial for the success of your data-driven game. This appendix outlines key best practices to guide you in creating a robust and scalable database that can handle the complexities of your game data.

1. Define Clear Objectives

Before diving into database design, clearly define the purpose of your database and the types of data you need to store. Identify the entities involved in your game (e.g., players, items, quests, enemies) and the relationships between them. This clarity will guide your design choices and ensure your database aligns with your game's needs.

2. Normalize Your Data

Normalization is the process of organizing data into logical tables and minimizing redundancy. It involves breaking down large tables into smaller, related tables and establishing relationships between them using foreign keys. This ensures data integrity, reduces storage space, and improves query performance.

- **Common Normal Forms:**

- **First Normal Form (1NF):** Eliminate repeating groups of data within a table.
- **Second Normal Form (2NF):** Remove redundant data that depends on only part of the primary key.
- **Third Normal Form (3NF):** Eliminate data that depends on non-key columns.

3. Choose Appropriate Data Types

Select the most suitable data type for each column in your tables. This ensures data integrity, optimizes storage space, and improves query efficiency. Consider factors like data range, precision, and potential for future changes when choosing data types.

4. Use Constraints Wisely

Constraints enforce data integrity and prevent invalid data from entering your database. Use constraints like NOT NULL, UNIQUE, PRIMARY KEY, FOREIGN KEY, and CHECK to define rules and relationships between your data.

5. Optimize for Performance

Design your database with performance in mind. Use indexing to speed up data retrieval, optimize queries to reduce database load, and consider caching frequently accessed data. Analyze query plans to identify and address performance bottlenecks.

6. Prioritize Security

Implement robust security measures to protect your database from unauthorized access and malicious attacks. Use strong passwords, parameterized queries, access control mechanisms, and encryption to safeguard your data.

7. Plan for Scalability

Consider how your database will scale as your game grows and attracts more players. Choose a database system that can handle increasing data volumes and user traffic. Consider techniques like data partitioning or sharding to distribute data across multiple servers.

8. Document Your Design

Document your database design, including table structures, relationships, constraints, and design decisions. This documentation will be invaluable for future maintenance, updates, and collaboration with other developers.

9. Use Visual Tools

Utilize visual tools like entity-relationship diagrams (ERDs) to model your database structure and visualize relationships between tables. These diagrams can help you identify potential design flaws or areas for improvement.

10. Test Thoroughly

Test your database design thoroughly before deploying your game. Populate the database with sample data and execute various queries to ensure data integrity, performance, and functionality.

11. Iterate and Refine

Database design is an iterative process. As your game evolves and your understanding grows, be prepared to refine your database schema, optimize queries, and adapt to changing requirements.

By following these best practices, you can create a robust, secure, and scalable database that forms a solid foundation for your data-driven game. Remember that careful planning and attention to detail in the design phase can save you time and effort in the long run and contribute to a more enjoyable and engaging gaming experience for your players.

www.ingramcontent.com/pod-product-compliance
Lightning Source LLC
LaVergne TN
LVHW051328050326
832903LV00031B/3424